汉语
日常交际中请求行为的微妙性

Delicacy in Requesting in Mandarin Chinese Mundane Conversations

刘 蜀 著

中国社会科学出版社

图书在版编目（CIP）数据

汉语日常交际中请求行为的微妙性 / 刘蜀著. — 北京：中国社会科学出版社，2025.4. —— ISBN 978-7-5227-4851-1

Ⅰ. H1

中国国家版本馆 CIP 数据核字第 202531HT01 号

出 版 人	赵剑英
责任编辑	张 浠
责任校对	姜志菊
责任印制	李寡寡

出　　版	中国社会科学出版社
社　　址	北京鼓楼西大街甲 158 号
邮　　编	100720
网　　址	http://www.csspw.cn
发 行 部	010－84083685
门 市 部	010－84029450
经　　销	新华书店及其他书店
印　　刷	北京明恒达印务有限公司
装　　订	廊坊市广阳区广增装订厂
版　　次	2025 年 4 月第 1 版
印　　次	2025 年 4 月第 1 次印刷
开　　本	710×1000　1/16
印　　张	14
插　　页	2
字　　数	225 千字
定　　价	78.00 元

凡购买中国社会科学出版社图书，如有质量问题请与本社营销中心联系调换
电话：010－84083683
版权所有　侵权必究

TABLE OF CONTENTS

CHAPTER ONE   INTRODUCTION ·················· (1)
   1.1   Research Object ·································· (1)
   1.2   Rationale of the Present Study ·················· (2)
   1.3   Delimitation of Delicacy ························· (4)
   1.4   Objectives of the Present Study ················ (8)
   1.5   Methodology of the Present Study ············· (9)
   1.6   Significance of the Present Study ··············· (10)
   1.7   Outline of the Study ····························· (12)

CHAPTER TWO   LITERATURE REVIEW ················ (13)
   2.1   Introduction ······································· (13)
   2.2   Requests in Pragmatics ·························· (13)
      2.2.1   Definitions of requests ······················· (13)
      2.2.2   Classifications of requests and their criteria ············ (14)
      2.2.3   Grammatical constructions of request forms ·············· (16)
      2.2.4   Politeness-related studies on requests ················ (17)
      2.2.5   Requests in cross-cultural pragmatics ················· (21)
   2.3   Requests in Conversation Analysis ·············· (24)
      2.3.1   Request sequences ·························· (24)
      2.3.2   Grammatical designs of the requesting turn ············· (27)

2.3.3 Requests and directives ……………………… (33)
2.3.4 Effects of reasons/accounts of requests ……………… (34)
2.3.5 Recruitment of assistance ……………………… (36)
2.3.6 Studies on requesting from other perspectives ………… (37)
2.4 Requests in Other Fields ……………………………… (38)
2.5 Delicacy ……………………………………………… (40)
2.6 Comments on the Existing Studies ……………………… (43)
2.7 Summary ……………………………………………… (44)

CHAPTER THREE RESEARCH METHODOLOGY ………… (45)
3.1 Origins and Development of CA ……………………… (45)
  3.1.1 Influence of Erving Goffman ……………………… (45)
  3.1.2 Influence of Harold Garfinkel ……………………… (46)
  3.1.3 Development and classification of CA ……………… (47)
3.2 The Scientificity of CA ……………………………… (51)
  3.2.1 Naturally occurring data ………………………… (51)
  3.2.2 The system of transcription ……………………… (52)
  3.2.3 A quasi-natural scientific approach ………………… (53)
  3.2.4 Contrastive analysis ……………………………… (54)
  3.2.5 Data session ……………………………………… (55)
3.3 Basic Notions of CA ………………………………… (56)
  3.3.1 Turn taking system ……………………………… (56)
  3.3.2 Sequence organization …………………………… (58)
  3.3.3 Preference organization ………………………… (67)
3.4 Research Procedures of the Present Study ……………… (69)
  3.4.1 Observation and question formulation ……………… (69)
  3.4.2 Data collection and transcription …………………… (70)
  3.4.3 Analysis ………………………………………… (70)
3.5 Summary ……………………………………………… (71)

TABLE OF CONTENTS

CHAPTER FOUR DELICACY IN SEQUENCE ORGANIZATION OF REQUESTING (72)

4.1 Delicacy in Pre-expansion of Request Sequence (72)
    4.1.1 Delicacy in pre-requests (73)
    4.1.2 Delicacy in pre-pres (79)
4.2 Delicacy in Goings-In-Front-Of-Requests (83)
    4.2.1 Delicacy in generic goings-in-front-of-requests (83)
    4.2.2 Delicacy in type-specific goings-in-front-of-requests (86)
4.3 Summary (92)

CHAPTER FIVE DELICACY IN TURN DESIGN OF REQUESTING (94)

5.1 Deferring the Requests (94)
    5.1.1 Turn initial delays (94)
    5.1.2 Other actions-prefaced requests (97)
5.2 Accounts (99)
5.3 Appreciation (102)
5.4 Index of a Distribution of Benefits and/or Costs Associated with Requesting (103)
    5.4.1 Minimal portrayal of requesting (104)
    5.4.2 Minimization of costs of requesting to requestees (109)
    5.4.3 Maximization of benefits of requesting to requesters (112)
5.5 Lexical-syntactic Formats of Requesting (114)
    5.5.1 Imperatives (115)
    5.5.2 Interrogatives (117)
    5.5.3 Declaratives (119)
5.6 Summary (122)

CHAPTER SIX THE DELICACY OF REQUESTING AND SOCIAL SOLIDARITY ……………………………… (124)

6.1　Introduction ……………………………………………… (124)
　6.1.1　Altruism ……………………………………………… (124)
　6.1.2　Social norms ………………………………………… (126)
　6.1.3　Social solidarity …………………………………… (129)
6.2　Altruism and Social Solidarity ………………………… (131)
　6.2.1　Altruism in requesting sequences ………………… (131)
　6.2.2　Altruism in turn designs of requesting ………… (137)
6.3　Social Norms and Social Solidarity …………………… (143)
　6.3.1　Requesting sequence and social norms ………… (144)
　6.3.2　Turn designs of requesting and social norms …… (161)
6.4　Delicacy, Altruism, Social Norms and Social Solidarity …… (175)
　6.4.1　Altruism: the intrinsic engine for delicacy ……… (176)
　6.4.2　Social norms: the realization of delicacy ………… (178)
　6.4.3　Social solidarity: the aim of being delicate ……… (180)
6.5　Summary …………………………………………………… (181)

CHAPTER SEVEN CONCLUSION …………………………… (183)

7.1　Findings and Contributions of the Present Study ……… (183)
7.2　Implications of the Present Study ……………………… (187)
7.3　Limitations of the Present Study ………………………… (187)
7.4　Suggestions for Further Study …………………………… (188)

REFERENCES ………………………………………………… (190)

APPENDIX TRANSCRIPTION CONVENTIONS …………… (212)

ACKNOWLEDGEMENT ……………………………………… (214)

目 录

第一章 前言 …………………………………………（1）
  1.1 研究对象 ………………………………………（1）
  1.2 选题依据 ………………………………………（2）
  1.3 微妙性 …………………………………………（4）
  1.4 研究目标 ………………………………………（8）
  1.5 研究方法 ………………………………………（9）
  1.6 研究意义 ………………………………………（10）
  1.7 内容提要 ………………………………………（12）

第二章 文献综述 ……………………………………（13）
  2.1 引言 ……………………………………………（13）
  2.2 请求在语用学中的研究 ………………………（13）
    2.2.1 请求的定义 ………………………………（13）
    2.2.2 请求的分类及划分标准 …………………（14）
    2.2.3 请求的语法形式研究 ……………………（16）
    2.2.4 请求与礼貌理论相关的研究 ……………（17）
    2.2.5 请求在跨文化语用学中的研究 …………（21）
  2.3 请求在会话分析中的研究 ……………………（24）
    2.3.1 请求序列 …………………………………（24）
    2.3.2 请求的话轮设计 …………………………（27）

2.3.3　请求与祈使 …………………………………… (33)
　　2.3.4　请求原因/解释的作用 ………………………… (34)
　　2.3.5　获助 …………………………………………… (36)
　　2.3.6　从其他角度对请求的研究 …………………… (37)
　2.4　请求在其他领域的研究 ………………………………… (38)
　2.5　微妙性 …………………………………………………… (40)
　2.6　对当前研究的简要评价 ………………………………… (43)
　2.7　小结 ……………………………………………………… (44)

第三章　研究方法 ………………………………………………… (45)
　3.1　会话分析的起源与发展 ………………………………… (45)
　　3.1.1　Erving Goffman 的影响 ………………………… (45)
　　3.1.2　Harold Garfinkel 的影响 ………………………… (46)
　　3.1.3　会话分析的发展与分类 ………………………… (47)
　3.2　会话分析的科学性 ……………………………………… (51)
　　3.2.1　自然会话为语料 ………………………………… (51)
　　3.2.2　转写体系 ………………………………………… (52)
　　3.2.3　似自然科学的研究方法 ………………………… (53)
　　3.2.4　对比分析 ………………………………………… (54)
　　3.2.5　语料分析与讨论 ………………………………… (55)
　3.3　会话分析的基本概念 …………………………………… (56)
　　3.3.1　话轮机制 ………………………………………… (56)
　　3.3.2　序列组织 ………………………………………… (58)
　　3.3.3　优先组织 ………………………………………… (67)
　3.4　研究步骤 ………………………………………………… (69)
　　3.4.1　观察语料与提出研究问题 ……………………… (69)
　　3.4.2　语料收集与转写 ………………………………… (70)
　　3.4.3　分析 ……………………………………………… (70)
　3.5　小结 ……………………………………………………… (71)

第四章　请求微妙性在序列组织中的构建 ……………………（72）
4.1　请求微妙性在请求序列的前扩展中的构建 ……………（72）
4.1.1　请求微妙性在请求前序列中的构建 ……………（73）
4.1.2　请求微妙性在请求预备前序列中的构建 ………（79）
4.2　请求微妙性在前序序列中的构建 ………………………（83）
4.2.1　请求微妙性在一般前序序列中的构建 …………（83）
4.2.2　请求微妙性在特定类型前序序列中的构建 ……（86）
4.3　小结 ………………………………………………………（92）

第五章　请求微妙性在话轮设计中的构建 ……………………（94）
5.1　请求的推迟出现 ……………………………………………（94）
5.1.1　话轮起始位置的拖延 ……………………………（94）
5.1.2　其他行为推迟请求的出现 ………………………（97）
5.2　解释 …………………………………………………………（99）
5.3　感谢 …………………………………………………………（102）
5.4　请求行为受益与付出的分布 ……………………………（103）
5.4.1　请求的弱化描述 …………………………………（104）
5.4.2　被请求者付出的最小化 …………………………（109）
5.4.3　请求者受益的最大化 ……………………………（112）
5.5　执行请求的不同语言形式 ………………………………（114）
5.5.1　祈使句 ……………………………………………（115）
5.5.2　疑问句 ……………………………………………（117）
5.5.3　陈述句 ……………………………………………（119）
5.6　小结 ………………………………………………………（122）

第六章　请求微妙性与社会和谐 ………………………………（124）
6.1　引言 ………………………………………………………（124）
6.1.1　利他主义 …………………………………………（124）
6.1.2　社会规范 …………………………………………（126）

  6.1.3 社会和谐 ···（129）
 6.2 利他主义与社会和谐 ···（131）
  6.2.1 利他主义在请求序列中的体现 ·······················（131）
  6.2.2 利他主义在请求话轮设计中的体现 ················（137）
 6.3 社会规范与社会和谐 ···（143）
  6.3.1 请求序列与社会规范 ····································（144）
  6.3.2 请求话轮设计与社会规范 ·····························（161）
 6.4 微妙性、利他主义、社会规范与社会和谐 ···············（175）
  6.4.1 利他主义:构建请求微妙性的内在引擎 ············（176）
  6.4.2 社会规范:构建请求微妙性的方式 ···················（178）
  6.4.3 社会和谐:构建请求微妙性的目标 ···················（180）
 6.5 小结 ···（181）

第七章 结语 ···（183）
 7.1 主要发现及贡献 ··（183）
 7.2 研究启示 ··（187）
 7.3 研究局限 ··（187）
 7.4 对进一步研究的建议 ···（188）

参考文献 ···（190）

附录 转写规则 ··（212）

致谢 ··（214）

CHAPTER ONE   INTRODUCTION

1.1   Research Object

Requesting, whose dictionary definition is "the action of asking for something formally and politely" (The Oxford Advanced Learner's Dictionary), is a social action frequently resorted to by social members in social interaction. It is common for one to ask for assistance from acquaintances and even strangers when she or he lacks the capability in fulfilling some task or is constrained by some physical (temporal or spacial), social or psychological conditions from performing some conduct by her/himself. The party who needs assistance is called the Requester and the party who provides assistance is called the Requestee. As a social action, requesting has four main features: (1) it is an initiating action which requires a response; (2) its response is either a granting or a refusal; (3) in terms of benefit and cost, the requester is the beneficiary and the requestee is the benefactor (Clayman and Heritage, 2014), namely, the requester is the one who benefits and the requestee is the one who pays out time, money, energy or something else to help the requester achieve what s/he wants and (4) in terms of the thing requested, requesting can be generally divided into request for object, request for action and request for information. Only the first two types are studied in the present study while the third type is attributed to the action of inquiry. The requesting sequence is the locus of observation of the present study.

It is said that requesting is at the core of how we manage social cohesion and solidarity (Drew & Couper-Kuhlen, 2014: 2). As we all know, when a request is issued, its recipient has the obligation to give a response, no matter it is a granting or a refusal. On the one hand, as a face-threatening act (Brown & Levinson, 1987), the very issuance of a request puts an imposition on its rec-ipient. If the request is granted, the requestee needs to make some cost to fulfill the task requested; if the request is rejected, the requestee runs the risk of offending the requester. On the other hand, the requester has to expose her/his lack of possession of something or inability to do something by her/himself to the requestee. In this sense, requesting is also not a favorable action for one to implement in order to maintain her/his "face" (Goffman, 1955). Therefore, it is a rather delicate issue to make a request while keeping the social relations between the requester and the requestee safe and sound. It is worthwhile to make a close observation of social interaction to unravel the mystery of the normativity of requesting. Driven by this curiosity, the present study intends to find out the normative ways of making a request by social members in which the delicacy of requesting is demonstrated. In a word, requesting sequences in talks-in-interaction are the locus of observation and the delicacy displayed in this type of action sequence is the focus of the present investigation.

1.2　Rationale of the Present Study

Requesting, as a ubiquitous social action, has drawn the attention of the researchers in sociolinguistics, pragmatics, cross-cultural communication, conversation analysis, etc. Request has been described as a face-threatening act to the face of both the requester and the requestee (Brown & Levinson, 1987) and lots of interactional, personal and social contingencies need to be dealt

CHAPTER ONE INTRODUCTION

with in request sequences (Vinkhuyzen & Szymanski, 2005). Research on requests has so far focused on inference rules and processes about how requests are understood from the perspective of the speech act theory, indirectness of request strategies relating to imposition, social distance and deference in terms of the politeness theory, contrastive studies on relationships between request strategies and politeness of eight languages in cross-cultural pragmatics, influences of social variables such as age, gender and identity, etc. on the choice of request strategies in sociolinguistics and the decisive role of requesters' assessment of entitlement and contingency surrounding granting of a request on the selection of turn designs of requesting in conversation analysis, etc. However, request has been studied as a single utterance statically in pragmatic and linguistic fields while the sequential development of interaction has been ignored. And little study has investigated requesting in Chinese from the perspective of turn design and sequence organization, etc. adopting the methodology of conversation analysis. So this study, taking conversation analysis as its research methodology, makes an empirical investigation into requesting in mundane conversation, to offer a comprehensive account of how requesting is initiated(including the sequence organization and turn design of requesting) and provides a dynamic picture of interactional details in requesting having been neglected in previous studies.

The present study is grounded on the following considerations: Firstly, requesting is a commonly resorted social action in our social life. We frequently request others and are requested by others to do something or we request something from others and are requested of something by others. Secondly, few studies of requests in Mandarin Chinese have used naturally-occurring conversations as their data. The data have been collected mainly by means of questionnaires, interviews, role plays and discourse completion tasks (Ren Wei, 2018; Zhang Shaojie & Wang Xiaotong, 1997), etc. Thirdly, the past studies mainly focused on the pragmatic strategies used by people speaking different languages. Fourthly, conversation analysis has seldom been used in the study of requests in Mandarin Chinese, thus the sequence organization and turn design of requesting in Chinese mundane conversations have not been touched upon. Fifthly, due to the commonness of requests in our social life, it is seldom regarded as a delicate issue to make a request. Lastly, when something is said to be delicate, delicacy is usually considered as the intrinsic feature of that topic, such as sex and death. Delicacy is seldom understood as being constructed by language users in talk-in-interaction. The aim of the present study is to demonstrate the complexity and contingency in making requests in terms of its sequence organization and turn design. It is an empirical study of requesting to find out evidences from naturally-occurring conversations to support the claims made by politeness theories, that is to say, requesting is a face-threatening act.

1.3 Delimitation of Delicacy

There has been a normally accepted assumption that some topics such as sex, illness and death are intrinsically delicate, sensitive, embarrassing and awkward, and are difficult to address in social interactions (Linell & Bredmar, 1996; Yu & Wu, 2015). This idea has led to speculations that delicacy may relate to the person whom these topics are concerned or to the social context where these topics are arising. The consideration as such is twofold. On the one hand, it would limit us to a social psychology of how people respond to "embarrassing" situations (Silverman, 2001: 119), which is elusive and hard to be inspected and the research achievement is, hence, up till now scarce due to the black box nature. On the other hand, it suggests that the delicacy or sensitivity of some topics is not so much intrinsic to the topic per se, but is rather contingent on social setting and the participants involved (Yu & Wu, 2015: 202), which provides minute details rea-

CHAPTER ONE   INTRODUCTION

dy for investigation and rigorous evidence for action ascription. It is the latter which is more fitted to the orientation in this research. In the light of this remarkable clue, it is widely accepted in the micro-study of interaction that a delicate matter or topic is locally produced and managed as the sequence unfolds. That is, something delicate or sensitive is displayed as being delicate or sensitive with certain person on certain local occasion through the way whether something being talked about is easy to be moved in or out (Jefferson, 1984a), whether something being talked about is directly presented (Walker, Drew & Local, 2011) or whether something being talked about involves changes of footing (Clayman, 1992) or elicitation of an opinion from the co-participants (Maynard, 1991), etc.

This study, in line with the idea that delicacy is an interactional phenomenon, focuses on delicacy in action, herein requesting, rather than delicacy of a topic or matter. As is common in delicate topics or matters, practices, often deployed to mark delicacy, as is shown in the literature, are expressive caution which is displayed by delays, perturbations, avoidances, mitigation, hedging, elaborations, story prefaces, depersonalizations and indirectness (Bergmann, 1992; Linell & Bredmar, 1996; Silverman, 1997), laughter (Haakana, 2001 & 2010), footing changes (Clayman, 1992), and category-bound activities or category-bound features (Silverman, 1987 & 1997), etc. These practices provide clues for participants (and observers or researchers) to distinguish what is being delicate and how such delicacy is presented.

Ex. 1 [PZD 17/XBQ/1: 0: 00]

Having achieved recognition and identification, Dong (东) asks the reason for the call. Instead of directly initiating a request, Qiong (琼) produces a multi-TCUs turn composed of an abandoned TCU, a pre-request, an account and another pre-request (Lines 04-07).

01 琼：   师 [兄我是徐琼你知道我吗?

02 东：   ［喂，
03 东：   嗯嗯，(.) 咋啦，
04 琼：   那个（.）那个（.）我:-你们实验室做土壤有没有
05   用过那个352硝基水杨酸呀=>我的实验做到一半儿
06   就差0.1克那个下午才送过来呢我这会就要用的<，
07   (.) 你们实验室有没有呀.
08   (0.5)
09 东：   哎:呀:好像有（.）好像有，
10 琼：   三:五:二硝基硝基水杨- 水水杨酸,=
11 东：   =嗯:好像有呢，
12   (0.7)
13 琼：   嗯::那在哪放（（按键音））能不能自己找一下=然后
14   我用完给你还- 马上就还回来.
15 东：   呃可以可以，你过去找吧. 呃，

In this example, there are some familiar and similar practices deployed in delicate topics: First, the demonstration of perturbations (including turn initial delay and self-repair) (Line 04); then the employment of two pre-requests progressively, which is separated by an account (Lines 04-07).

It can be noticed that with the issue of perturbations, what is to be forthcoming not only is approached in a hesitating manner and with expressive caution (Silverman, 2001), but is delayed to some extent simultaneously. Thus, it is evident that perturbations produced by Qiong is dealing with the issue at hand as delicate. What follows is the availability of the requested object checked by two pre-requests progressively. The first question asks whether the target object has been used in Dong's lab., which is the precondition to the second one. At this moment, this question can be understood in two ways. It may be a pre-request of the requested object. It also may be a pre-consultation of the target object. The subsequent account provides all the background information including the reason, urgency and amount of the

CHAPTER ONE INTRODUCTION

required target object. It not only serves as grounds for asking the prior question and clarifying its function – pre-request, but also implies her trouble and projects a possible requesting to be forthcoming. Thereby, she is possibly soliciting an offer. Then it proceeds to another pre-request, which explicitly asks whether there is the targeted object in Dong's lab.

Taken together, the requester delicately and cautiously prepares the grounds for initiating a prospective request by either pre-requests, account, or both, all of which sequentially defers the delivery of the upcoming request and provides a slot for possible offer-provision. Besides the sequence prior to the request turn, the turn that implements the action of requesting also demonstrates requesters' delicate or subtle management of their requesting, as is displayed in Ex. 2.

Ex. 2 ［PZD 17/LAX/4：0：00］
01　　　　（0.5）
02　雄：　喂老彭,
03　东：　↓喂.
04　　　　（0.7）
05　雄：　你人来了没h.
06　东：　没呢.
07　　　　（1.4）
08　雄：　没:呢:=
09　东：　=嗯:(.)怎么了?
10　　　　（1.6）
11　雄：　噢:::我找个篮球,
12　　　　（0.7）
13　雄：　［噢:看到了.
14　东：　［(嗯)
15　东：　对哇你们(.)［(就到)我宿舍拿吧.

Based on the evidence that the requestee（东）is unavailable provided by pre-request (Lines 05-06), the requester Xiong (雄) does not initiate his request until the requestee's inquiry about his reason for pre-request. Here it can be observed that the request is implemented by declaratives in a mitigated or attenuated way (Line 11). The choice of declaratives shows the requester's highly attentive or sensitive to unfolding sequence on a turn-by-turn basis. Instead of using the verb *to borrow* ("借"), Xiong chooses the verb *to find* ("找"), by which minimal nature of his request is conveyed (Clayman & Heritage, 2014) and the easiness of the action being requested is connoted. As with some delicate conversational practices exploited in delicate topics or matters, the occurrence of softened words, one way of mitigation, is evidence of doing being delicate in requesting.

As demonstrated in the above examples, delicacy in requesting is locally constructed and managed as requesters involve in the unfolding sequence. It is obvious that the practices used to construct or mark delicacy are the same as those used either in delicate topics or matters or in dispreferred actions, such as delay, account and mitigation, etc. However, practices for doing being delicate are not limited to those identified in the previous research. Based on the data, some particular practices, which are not available in the existing literature, will be further examined under scrutiny in this study.

1.4 Objectives of the Present Study

Request is considered a face-threatening act (Brown & Levinson, 1987). It threatens the negative face of its recipients who are free from imposition and it also threatens speakers' positive face when the response to one's request is anything less than a granting. Therefore, issues of not only face but also social solidarity are at stake when a request is made. It is no wonder that there is a widespread belief that request is a potential delicate matter. So it is of great interest that how people make a request avoiding threatening faces of both sides as far as possible and how they orient to such a sensitive action. In order to prove delicacy is not a pre-determined feature of requests but an interactional consequence constructed by requesters, the present study will be guided by the following research questions:

(1) Why is requesting perceived as being delicate in terms of its sequence organization?

(2) Why is requesting perceived as being delicate in terms of its turn design?

(3) What are the forces driving requesters to construct or present requesting in the way as it is?

Answers to these questions also provide us a detailed understanding of interactional dynamics during the course of making a request missing in the previous studies.

1.5 Methodology of the Present Study

Conversation Analysis is an inductive, micro-analytic and predominantly qualitative method for studying language as it is used in social interaction (Hoey & Kendrick, 2018). Different from other methods, conversation analysis requires that data must be naturally occurring interactions, which are audiotaped or video-recorded. Transcripts of data follow the transcription conventions invented by Gail Jefferson to capture details about how the actual talk is delivered as detailed as possible. Although reading transcripts has similar effects with listening to the audio recordings, conversation analysts never consider transcripts a replacement for the data (Hepburn & Bolden, 2013).

With its focus on language as a vehicle for social action (Drew & Heritage, 1992: 16), conversation analysis seeks to uncover how actions are constructed or constituted through linguistic resources and how actions are managed interactionally and sequentially and recognized to be the actions that talk is designed to conduct or "perform" (Drew, 2013a: 3). In other words, the interplay between turn designs and sequence organization by which social actions are implemented in the particular sequential placement of a sequence organization is the major concern of conversation analysis, from the perspective of how participants display for one another their understanding of "what is going on" (Hutchby & Wooffitt, 1998: 15), rather than on assumptions of analysts. So here the basic concepts – social action, sequence organization and turn design in conversation analysis need mentioning. Social action refers to what participants are doing in turns-at-talk, which is accomplished in sequences. Sequence organization refers to how successive turns link up to form coherent courses of action (Hoey & Kendrick, 2018). The basic unit of this organization is the adjacency pair. Turn design refers to how speakers construct a turn to implement an action, which is recognized as the implemented action by recipients based on speakers' construction of the turn (Drew, 2013b).

The advantage of the methodology of conversation analysis is that it is a naturalistic observational discipline that could deal with the details of social actions rigorously, empirically and formally (Schegloff & Sacks, 1973). Different from other approaches to talk-in-interaction, conversation analysis is not theory-driven, that is to say, the findings made by conversation analysis are not to propose theories but to describe what the interactants exactly do in interaction. The aim of conversation analysis is to uncover the practices or common methods people use to do social actions (Drew, 2013a).

1.6　Significance of the Present Study

The present study contributes to the research on requests in the following aspects:

Firstly, the data of the present study are naturally-occurring mundane conversations of our real life. The data are transcripts of real-life conversations

CHAPTER ONE INTRODUCTION

which keep the details of interaction as meticulously as possible. Thus it is a mirror of the real talk-in-interaction. Different from data collected through interviews, questionnaires, discourse completion tasks or from TV series etc., the naturally-occurring conversations have been least affected by the research settings because "… the materials we worked with exhibited orderliness they did so not only for us, indeed not in the first place for us (conversation analysts), but for the co-participants who had produced them" (Schegloff & Sacks, 1973: 290).

Secondly, sequential context of requesting is underscored in the present study while what is considered in the previous studies is usually the ethnographic context. Conversation progresses on the turn-by-turn, moment-by-moment basis. The trajectory of talk-in-interaction is contingent on the conversational contributions made by the participants of each turn instead of by the genders, ages, educational backgrounds, etc. of the participants. So the attention paid to the requesting sequence instead of merely the request turn will provide a brand-new interpretation to request-making in Chinese conversations.

Thirdly, the details of the turn designs of the requesting turn are meticulously described and analyzed in the present study, including not only its syntactic formats but also various delays, minimizers of the cost and maximizers of the benefit, accounts, appreciations, etc. The past research on pragmatic strategies of making requests mainly focuses on the syntactic formats chosen by interactants. The real picture of requesting is far more complex than what have been found in the existing research.

Fourthly, the delicacy of requesting is interpreted in the present study from the perspective of social solidarity. Orienting to social norms is a universal social phenomenon and is the reason why society works in an orderly manner. At the same time, people are altruistic rather than selfish in their social contact with others. Social cohesion and social solidarity are cooperatively achieved by members of society. The past research stresses the cultural peculiarity while the present study emphasizes universality in making requests because social solidary is the common goal pursued by all societies.

Lastly, the present study also has its practical value in terms of teaching Chinese as a foreign language. Grammar and lexicons are the two focuses in foreign language teaching. The teaching materials edited in the textbooks come from either speculation or literary works. Few textbooks use language data collected from real-life conversations. The role played by sequences of conversation has been overlooked in the past foreign language teaching. Thus, the findings of the present study contributes to both teaching and studying Chinese as a foreign language and promotes mutual understanding between native speakers and foreign learners of Chinese language.

All in all, the present study makes a contribution to the growing body of research not only on requesting but also on Chinese social interactions as a whole.

1.7 Outline of the Study

This study consists of seven chapters. Chapter One presents a brief introduction to the research object, rationale, objectives, methodology and significance of this study. Chapter Two provides a comprehensive review of the existing studies of requests in various languages from different perspectives. Chapter Three introduces Conversation Analysis as the research methodology of this study. Its origin, basic concepts, research procedures, its scientificity, etc. are included in this chapter. Chapter Four and Chapter Five demonstrate the construction of delicacy in requesting from the perspective of sequence organization and turn design respectively. Chapter Six is devoted to the interpretation of delicacy in requesting in terms of social solidarity, social norms and altruism. Chapter Seven is the conclusion summing up findings, contributions, implications and limitations of the present study as well as suggestions for future research.

CHAPTER TWO   LITERATURE REVIEW

2.1   Introduction

Requesting is a widely investigated topic involving more than ten languages in several language-related disciplines. This chapter will be concerned with the review of the previous literature on requests, from the following dimensions: pragmatics, sociolinguistics, second language acquisition, cognitive linguistics and conversation analysis, which offers a clear picture of the existing studies on requests.

2.2   Requests in Pragmatics

Request, as a speech act, has been widely studied in pragmatics. It has been defined and classified from various angles. The pragmatic strategies employed to carry out requests have been investigated. The cross-linguistic comparison has also been made to find out the similarities and differences of doing request in different cultures.

2.2.1   Definitions of requests

According to Searle (1969), requests are directive speech acts satisfying certain felicity conditions (that is, preparatory condition, sincerity condition, propositional content condition and essential condition), indicating that speakers try to make recipients do an action and speakers presume that recipients can do it for him or her. However, it is not clear whether recipients will help him or her (1969: 66), based on which with some adjustment, Searle makes another definition, that is, a request is an attempt by the speaker to get the hearer to do something. They may be very modest attempts as when I invite you to do it, or they may be very fierce attempts as when I insist that you do it (1979: 13). Similar to this definition, Ellis (1994) holds that "requests are attempts on the part of a speaker to get the hearer to perform or to stop performing some kind of action" (1994: 167). Besides, other scholars give requests different definitions from different perspectives. Blum-Kulka et al (1985) consider that requests, as pre-event acts, express speakers' expectation of hearers in respect of some verbal or nonverbal prospective actions.

2.2.2 Classifications of requests and their criteria

In addition to definitions, a study of classifications and their relevant criteria allows us to have a fuller understanding of requests. In this respect, what Austin (1962), Ervin-Tripp (1977), Gibbs (1998), Leech (1983), Lyons (1977), Searle (1979) and Searle & Vanderveken (1985) have done deserves our attention. All the above scholars' works benefit from the ordinary language philosopher J. L. Austin's (1962) speech act theory. His basic idea is that saying is doing. By saying human are performing some actions, which are further analyzed into three component acts, namely, locutionary, illocutionary and perlocutionary acts. He further classifies illocutionary acts into five groups: verdictives, exercitives, commissives, behavities, and expositives. Requests are put under exercitives, defined as the exercising of powers, right, or influence

(Austin, 1962: 150). To overcome several weaknesses in Austin's categorization, Searle (1976) revises his taxonomy into a new list: representatives, directives, commissives, expressives, and declarations. He (1979) groups requests together with commands and orders into directives whose illocutionary point is to get the hearer to do something. Lyons (1977) and Leech (1983) both subsume requests and commands into the category of directives. However, we should notice that although in the same group, they are different from each other. The former allow the hearer to refuse to comply with while the latter do not. There are researchers like Searle and Vanderveken (1985) and Tsui (2000) holding the similar idea that requests leave the option for hearers to refuse. In addition to what the above scholars have done, i.e. to subsume requests under different categories, other scholars differentiate requests into different categories. According to Liao Chao-chih (1997), requests are classified into three types: obligatory requests, right-type requests and altruistic requests. Obligatory requests are used when the requestee has the obligation to do what is requested. Right-type requests are used when the requester has the right to ask the requestee to do what is requested. Altruistic requests are used in a donation situation, where there is neither a requester nor a requestee. From the perspective of speaker's action, addressee's action and both speaker and addressee's action, Tsui (2000) divides requestives into five groups: requests for permission, requests for offer, requests for action, requests for invitation and joint action.

To sum up, most of the above studies are further development in light of speech act theory and all the scholars except Austin group requests into the type of directives aiming to get the recipient to do something. How to classify requests is vital for us not only because it offers us some ways of how scholars understand requests differently but also because it offers us some guidelines of how different request strategies are employed correspondingly. Before we move to the section of request strategies, some studies on grammatical constructions of requests are reviewed first.

2.2.3 Grammatical constructions of request forms

With regard to grammatical constructions of requests, scholars are almost in agreement with Sifianou's opinion that requests can be performed with a variety of constructions, such as imperatives, interrogatives, declaratives, negatives and elliptical structures (1992: 125-157). However, they give different interpretations related to the issues about different choices of the above listed constructions. In English, it is inappropriate and unacceptable for people to make a request by direct imperatives which more suit to commands or instructions (Lyons, 1968) because imperatives are labeled as downright impolite (Clark & Schunk, 1980; Wardhaugh 1985) and they are face-threatening speech acts (Brown & Levinson, 1987) and at risk of disobedience (Leech, 1983). Besides, imperatives are the least polite constructions when compared with declaratives and interrogatives (Lakoff, 1977: 101; Leech, 1983: 119). But researchers from non-English speaking countries hold different ideas. In Greek, imperatives can be used to express both command and desire and wish (Triandafillides, 1978). In Russian, many more direct imperatives are considered polite usage than in English (Thomas, 1983). According to Zhang and Wang (1997), the Chinese often deploy imperatives to make a request among in-groups, such as family members, close friends, but infrequently among strangers. Furthermore, Larkin and O'Malley (1973) find that there are some situations where imperatives are used appropriately in English when requests are made, like advertisements, giving directions and keeping efficiency.

As for interrogatives, "can/could" requests are considered more polite than the "will/would" ones in that the former aims at the question about the hearer's ability to grant the request, whereas the latter aims to figure out the

CHAPTER TWO   LITERATURE REVIEW

hearer's willingness to comply with the request (Leech, 1983). Another grammatical construction often used is declaratives consisting of two categories – need statements and hints. Need statements are directly and explicitly statement of one's need. Contrary to need statements, hints quite indirectly express one's request in the declarative. Because they need interpretation on the part of the hearer, hints seem to be polite and the hearer can make a rejection based on his/her understanding of hints deliberately (Liu, 2003; Fan, 2011).

Requests expressed in negatives seem to be more polite than that in interrogatives (Green, 1975), which is supported by Stubbs' opinion that negative constructions are often used to mark politeness in discourse (Stubbs, 1983: 113). Ellipsis with no complete grammatical structures is a special form of requests, which requires the hearer to interpret the speaker's intention by (non-)linguistic information, context or shared knowledge between the participants (Liu, 2003; Fan, 2011). Ervin-Tripp's example (e.g. *Coffee, black.*) (1976: 30) is a case in point.

Having reviewed the definitions of requests, their classifications and relevant criteria, and the five types of grammatical constructions to perform requests in pragmatics, now we move to the politeness-related studies on requests.

2.2.4 Politeness-related studies on requests

Many scholars maintain that politeness is a good starting point to analyze requests. In terms of Goffman's face work (1955 & 1967), recipients' face is threatened by requests. He defines face as the positive social value a speaker claims for oneself. It usually consists of two kinds of particular wants: one, want to be unimpeded, free from imposition by others, the other, want to be approved of in certain respects. Based on the face work of Goffman (1955), Brown and Levinson (1978 & 1987) propose the politeness theory, an influential research angle about indirectness of requests. They hold that requesting is a face-threatening act, which can be interpreted as impingement on their freedom of action (Brown & Levinson, 1978 & 1987). At the same time, requesters' positive face would be threatened when a request is rejected and requestees' negative face would be threatened due to the imposition brought about by a request. They (1978) put forward five super-strategies of politeness in requests. These strategies range from the lowest level to the highest one in terms of different scales of politeness. They are: (a) a speaker may perform the request "boldly", with no acknowledgement of the hearer's face wants; (b) a speaker may perform the request while acknowledging the hearer's positive face wants and using positive politeness strategies labeled by Brown and Levinson (1978: 106); (c) a speaker might perform the request with the desire not to be impeded and imposed upon, acknowledging the hearer's negative face wants; (d) a speaker may "go off-record", performing the request in a vague manner (e.g. by offering hints), which may result in a misinterpretation as some other act and (e) performing no request and gaining no goal. Theoretically, speakers should use the more polite strategies when making a request with seriousness. However, practically, with all factors considered and weighted up and to reduce the cost of the strategies, speakers do not choose strategies that are more polite than necessary.

To address the question of what kind of requests is more polite, Clark and Schunk (1980) list six categories of request from the most polite to the least one: permission, imposition, ability, memory, commitment and obligation. In the case of permission, the speaker makes a request by asking for the hearer's permission (e.g. May I ask you who the dean is?). The category of imposition means that the speaker attends to the hearer's negative face by using terms to imply her/his thought about imposition (e.g. Would it too much trouble to tell me who the dean is?). The category of ability means that the ability of the hearer is challenged by the speaker (e.g. Can you tell me who the dean is?). In terms of memory, the speaker makes a request by asking the hearer to repeat the information to check her/his memory of having done something (e.g. Did I ask you who the dean is?). As for the category of commitment, the speaker challenges the hearer's willingness for a request (e.g. Do you want to tell me who the dean is?). The last one is obligation, in which the hearer's obligation is questioned (e.g. Shouldn't you tell me who the dean is?). Based on a quantitative research on the relative politeness rankings of 30 Mandarin linguistic forms of the core element "把门关上", Liao (1982) summarizes five patterns of Chinese request forms and their relative politeness rankings, as follows (Liao, 1982: 30):

(a) An interrogative sentence is more deferential and polite than the corresponding imperative form. For example, "能不能麻烦你把门关上?" (Can I trouble you to close the door?) is judged more polite than "麻烦你把门关上。" (Trouble you to close the door.). (b) An embedded sentence form is more deferential and polite than the corresponding non-embedded form. For example, "麻烦你把门关上, 好吗?" (Trouble you to close the door, all right?) is judged more polite than "你把门关上, 好吗?" (You, close the door, all right?). (c) An interrogative formed by an imperative request + modal-*ma* ("吗") tag is judged more polite than the corresponding one formed by an imperative sentence + modal-not-modal tag. For example, "麻烦你把门关上, 好吗?" (Trouble you to close the door, all right?) is more polite than "麻烦你把门关上, 好不好?" (Trouble to close the door, all right or not?). (d) The embedded *mafan* ("麻烦") sentence is judged more polite than the corresponding one with embedded – *qing* ("请"). For example, "能不能麻烦你把门关上?" (Can I trouble you to close the door?) is more polite than "能不能请你把门关上?" (Can I ask you to close the door?). And (e) an imperative request with *ni* is presumed to be more polite than the corresponding form without it. For example, "麻烦你把门关上" (Trouble you to close the door.) is more polite than "麻烦把门关

上" (Trouble to close the door.).

In Trosborg's opinion, a request is both an illocutionary act and an impositive act. The former means that a speaker (requester) conveys to a hearer (requestee) that s/he wants the requestee to perform an act, which is for the benefit of the speaker. The act may be a request for non-verbal goods and services, i.e. a request for an object, an action, etc. or for verbal goods and services, i.e. a request for information (Trosborg, 1995: 187) and the latter means that the requester imposes on the requestee when asking somebody to do her/him a favor or demanding goods or services. The degree with which the requester intrudes on the requestee, referred to as degree of imposition, may vary from small favors to demanding acts (Trosborg, 1995: 188).

As some researchers study how to make requests more polite, for requests impose on recipients to some extent, others work on strategies to make requests more acceptable from the perspective of (in)directness (Searle, 1976; Ervin-Tripp, 1977; Blum-Kulka, 1989, etc.).

As Searle states (1976), requests can be more or less direct. The directness here relates to the extent to which speakers' illocutionary intent is apparent from the locution. It is related to politeness, which does not mean that the concept of directness would be coextensive with politeness. Ervin-Tripp's findings show that Anglo-Americans use five categories of request strategies: (a) need or desire statements, e.g. "I need a match", directed to subordinates mainly; (b) imperatives, e.g. "Give me a match", directed to subordinates or solitary equals; (c) embedded imperatives, e.g. "Could you give me a match?" directed to non-solitary interlocutors or those of different status ranking to the speaker; (d) permissive directives, e.g. "May I have a match?" directed to non-solitary interlocutors or possibly those of superior rank; (e) hints, e.g. "The matches are all gone" (1977: 166-170). These five strategies make it possible that recipients' could refuse speakers' request, especially among friends and family members. According to Blum-Kulka

(1989), request strategies including nine sub-types are classified into direct, conventionally indirect and non-conventionally indirect, in terms of degrees of indirectness. And Blum-Kulka's viewpoint is also supported by Zhang Shaojie & Wang Xiaotong (1997) and Liu Guohui (2003).

2.2.5 Requests in cross-cultural pragmatics

In this section we will review research on requests in cross-cultural pragmatics, which has made great contributions to the study on requests. One of the most well-known projects is the Cross-cultural Speech Act Realization Project (CCSARP) (Blum-Kulka & Olshtain, 1984; Blum-Kulka, et al, 1989a). This project was carried out in an attempt to compare inter-lingual and intralingual realization patterns of requests and apologies across seven languages, five non-native speaker populations, and three national varieties of English (American English [AmE], Australian English, and British English [BrE]) (Flöck, 2016: 61). Data used in the project are elicited using Discourse Completion Task (DCT) consisting of short descriptions of sixteen situations including variables of social distance and relative status of the speaker and hearer, which are followed by incomplete dialogues to elicit the aimed speech acts. DCT is translated into multiple languages for the targeted research. Research within the framework is centered on the following three aspects.

2.2.5.1 Studies on request strategies and realizations

According to Blum-Kulka et al. (1989b), requests consist of a head act and a number of modification strategies including alerts and supportive moves and occurring either the head act internally or externally with functions of mitigating or aggravating. In terms of the head act, nine strategy types are identified and three directness levels are distinguished from direct, conventionally indirect to non-conventionally indirect (also referred as hints)

(Blum-Kulka et al., 1989a). Based on the DCT and the taxonomy of directness levels, a number of investigations of requests have been carried out across multiple languages and cultures over more than twenty years. There have been some common findings among different researchers. That is, there is a preference for conventionally indirect head act strategy (Blum-Kulka, 1989; Blum-Kulka & House, 1989; Faerch & Kasper, 1989; Zhang & Wang, 1997; Fukushima, 2000; Breuer & Geluykens, 2007; Barron, 2008; Lin, 2009; Ogiermann, 2009). Although the qualified result seems to be omnipresent, there also exists divergence of this conclusion. House and Kasper (1981) find out that requests in German are more direct than those in British English. A similar result is also observed by Ogiermann (2009) who reports that directness levels are continually rising from English to German, Polish and Russian. Likewise, in Reiter's research (2000), there is a higher number of direct head acts in Spanish requests than in British English requests. Besides, there are some findings contrary to the previous conclusion, for instance, Lee-Wong (1994 & 2000) reports that the direct strategy is prevailed in requests in Chinese, which is supported by Huang (1996) and Gao (1999). By comparison of requests between native speakers of Taiwanese Mandarin and American English, Huang (1996) argues that the direct request strategy is used more frequently by speakers of Taiwanese Mandarin than by American English speakers. Gao (1999) claims that direct requests are preferred in Chinese. In Economidou-Kogetsidis' studies on requests in British English (2010 & 2013), a lower usage on conventional indirectness is observed. The explanation for this result is that the setting in the DCT in the study (2013) is a business context where informants are more suitable to perform requests more directly.

In addition to what have been discussed above, some scholars pay their attention to modification strategies. The dominant position of internal mitigators is confirmed by Faerch and Kasper (1989) and Barron (2008) because internal mitigators are shorter and less complex and more easily to be attached to an utterance than external mitigators. And internal mitigators can avoid a potential problem to an interaction triggered by higher complexity of external mitigators as well (Faerch & Kasper, 1989). While in Barron's opinion, it is caused by contextual variation in her two groups of informants. In contrast to these studies, a preference for external mitigations over internal ones is observed in Reiter's research (2000) and Breuer and Geluykens' study (2007). Some researchers also explore upgraders in requests, such as House and Kasper (1981), Aijmer (1996) and Barron (2008). They found that the addition of *please* serves a multifunctional role – to function as an upgrader or a mitigator to requests in non-standard situations or in standard situations respectively (Flöck, 2016).

2.2.5.2 Studies on politeness and indirectness

Another focus in CCSARP is the relationship between indirectness and politeness in requests. Their findings show that indirectness does not imply politeness. Hints can be perceived as impolite due to a lack of pragmatic clarity, though it is the most indirect request strategy, while the highest level of politeness is the conventionally indirect strategy (Blum-Kulka et al., 1989a). The following researchers also have the similar findings, Holtgraves & Yang (1990), Zhang (1995), Felix-Brasdefer (2005), Marti (2006) and Ogiermann (2009). So the relationship between politeness and indirectness in previous studies cannot be treated as universal.

2.2.5.3 Studies on social variables

Research with the framework of CCSARP is also carried out on social variables including power, distance and imposition, proposed in Brown & Levinson's politeness theory and other variables such as gender, age (Blum-Kulka et al., 1985; Hill et al., 1986; Holtgraves & Yang, 1990; Lee-Wong, 1994 & 2000; Fukushima, 1996 & 2000; Zhang & Wang, 1997; Reiter, 2000; Rue & Zhang, 2008; Economidou-Kogetsidis, 2010). In these studies no universal agreement is reached. The influence on requests is the result of interaction among the three variables and other variables. Besides, the relative weight of these variables is different according to different cultures. Therefore, further research needs to be made in future.

2.3 Requests in Conversation Analysis

Considerable studies have been conducted on requests with the research methodology of Conversation Analysis in different directions, including responses to requests with different features which differentiate preferred responses from dispreferred ones in early stage (Heritage, 1984a; Schegloff, 2007), request sequences (Keisanen & Rauniomaa, 2012; Li Li & Ma Wen, 2016; Taleghani-Nikazm, 2006, etc.), grammatical designs of the request turn (Curl & Drew, 2008; Heinemann, 2006; Lindström, 2005; Zinken, & Ogiermann, 2013, etc.), reasons for requests (Baranova & Dingemanse, 2016; Taleghani-Nikazm, 2006, etc.) and recruitment (Drew & Couper-Kuhlen, 2014; Kendrick & Drew, 2016)

2.3.1 Request sequences

Previous studies on request sequences in the field of conversation analysis have mainly focused on turn formats of pre-requests (Taleghani-Nikazm, 2006), sequences prior to pre-requests and requests (Taleghani-Nikazm, 2006), sequences (including pre-requests) prior to requests in face-to-face interaction (Keisanen & Rauniomaa, 2012) and sequence organization of pre-requests (Rossi, 2015), responses to requests (Couper-Kuhlen, et al., 2011; Rauniomaa & Keisanen, 2012; Steensig & Heinemann, 2014) and requests in public service (Li Li & Ma Wen, 2016).

In Taleghani-Nikazm's study (2006), from the two aspects of position

CHAPTER TWO LITERATURE REVIEW

and composition, how turns at talk are recognized as pre-requests and how they and the subsequent talk occasion the following contingent requests are explored. Three turn formats of the pre-request are demonstrated: pre-requests (1) in the form of an inquiry which checks the likelihood of grantability of the projected request, (2) in the form of accounts which could elicit an offer and (3) in the form of mentioning likes which also receives an offer. Focusing on the sequential context in which requests occur, Taleghani-Nikazm (2006) also explores another aspect of request sequences, i. e. initiating request sequences, which refers to the talk that occurs as prefatory components to pre-requests and requests at turn beginnings and then displays how requests are introduced as a new activity. In terms of the information they carry, prefatory components to pre-requests and requests are classified into four categories, from the most "non-specific" prefatory components to the "most-specific" ones. All the four categories of prefatory components serve an interactional function – to signal the initiation of a new activity, which has been occasioned by the prior talk, and to project the subsequent talk as well. The analysis shows that the request sequences can be either introduced gradually by topical connection of the pre-request or request turn to the previous turn or abruptly with disconnection from the previous talk into the ongoing conversation. Besides, he demonstrates that turn beginning designs are used as the earliest resource for projecting the extending turn shape and the action being performed by the upcoming turn. And grammatical structures of a language are treated as one of the fundamental resource to anticipate the design of the unfolding turn and its ultimate implemented action.

Similar to Taleghani-Nikazm's work (2006), Keisanen and Rauniomaa (2012) focus on sequences immediately prior to the verbal request turn, which are termed as pre-beginnings. Because their data are based on face-to-face interactions, their findings are different from those of audio recordings. They find that resources such as gestures, material objects in the surrounding space, and movement and the positioning of participants are utilized to organize participation and deal with contingencies relating to requests in the phase of pre-beginnings to initiate requests.

From the perspective of sequential analysis of the pre-request format *hai x* in Italian, Rossi (2015) demonstrates the organization of this pre-request. From responses to it, *hai x* is judged as a pre-request. The immediate granting of the projected request is preferred over the go-ahead response to a pre-request, for the go-ahead response more or less defers granting of the upcoming request. Since *hai x* transparently projects the upcoming request, the fulfillment of the request is selected over a go-ahead response, which breaks progressivity between the first pair part and granting of the action initiated by it. In this sense, the *hai x* pre-request is expanded by a go-ahead response, which is a special property exhibited in *hai x* sequences. But this expansion is different from expansions such as pre-rejections and pre-disagreement. The second property of *hai x* sequences is that blocking responses are made with no features of dispreferred responses.

In addition to the above Rossi's studies on responses to pre-requests (Rossi, 2015), some research pays attention to responses to requests. Comparing different linguistic structures to comply with requests, Couper-Kuhlen, et al. (2011) propose that the speaker is committed more to fulfilling the request, when s/he uses the more complex structures. Rauniomaa & Keisanen (2012) identify two multimodal formats responses – immediate embodied fulfillment, and verbal acceptance plus (future) fulfillment, to requests for transferring of objects or service. The former is a reflection of immediacy and ease of fulfillment, while the latter indicates that the request will be accomplished in a near or more distant future, for there is another activity which needs to be implemented before the fulfillment of the request. The import of this study is the constitutive role played by embodied responses in the formation of request sequences in face-to-face interactions. Steensig and Heinemann (2014) take full clause formats (with or without a modal verb) responses to remote requests, namely, requests to be granted in the future, in Danish interactions as subjects at a finer level of granularity, showing that three forms are all designed as committed to doing the requested action, but differ in interactionally relevant ways, by which requestees display their commitment and orientation to the requested action differently. Responses without modal verbs are used to indicate that the requested action is treated as a given and an appropriate action to be carried out, while responses with modal verbs (including verbs of obligation and concession) are considered an indication that although the requested action is not appropriate, it will be complied with as well. In Li Li and Ma Wen's study (2016), characteristics of request sequences in Chinese public service call – frequent appearance of insert expansions and non-minimal post-expansions, which occur after both dispreferred and preferred responses, are generalized and epistemic asymmetry and interactants' institutional identities are found to explain this phenomenon.

2.3.2 Grammatical designs of the requesting turn

Compared to investigations on request sequences, more effort has been paid to reconsider syntactic formats to design the requesting turn. One reason may be that different languages provide interactants different syntactic formats to make a request. Maybe this is because requesting is traditionally considered a dispreferred and delicate social action (Heritage, 1984a; Levinson, 1983; Robinson & Bolden, 2010; Schegloff, 1990 & 2007; Taleghni-Nikazm, 2006).

Kendrick and Drew (2014) discuss the putative preference for offering over requesting and propose that this putative preference is untenable. They also discuss the relationship between offering and requesting. One kind of response to offering could be requesting which occurs after offering and could indicate acceptance of offering as well. A report or display of problems, some kind of an alternative to requesting, can occasion an offer. Offering, especially in multiparty interactions for some shareable objects, can occasion requesting.

2.3.2.1 Entitlement and contingency

Entitlement and contingency are found to be factors that play a part in how request turns are designed. Studies relate to these two factors including those by Antaki and Kent (2012), Curl and Drew (2008), Heinemann (2006), Lindsröm (2005) and Vinkhuyzen and Szymanski (2005). Lindsröm (2005) and Heinemann (2006) show that selections of syntactic structures to make requests are linked to entitlement when interactions between home help assistants and elderly care recipients in Swedish and Danish respectively. In Swedish, with an imperative request, care recipients orient to their request as one that they are entitled to make. In contrast, with an interrogative request, care recipients orient to their request as one that they are not entitled to make. In Danish, care recipients' high entitlement toward the requested task is displayed by the negative interrogatives, which are strengthened by the choice of verb and formulated in terms of recipients' willingness. Care recipients' low entitlement toward the requested task is displayed by positive interrogatives, which are mitigated and formulated in terms of recipients' ability. In a similar vein, Curl and Drew (2008) who compare requesting in casual daily calls and out-of-hours calls to doctors, argue that *I wonder if* prefaced requests are found to display requesters' orientation to high contingency and low entitlement. By contrast, requesters orient to high entitlement and low contingency by requests formulated with modal verbs, (say, *can/could/would*). The choice of request formats displays requesters' assessment of entitlement and contingency associated with the granting of a request. Their findings are congruent with Vinkhuyzen and Szymanski's findings (2005) and are supported by Antaki and Kent

(2012).

2.3.2.2 Ownership and entitlement

Ownership, in addition to entitlement, is an important factor in object requests between family members and friends. Several studies reveal a number of situation-specific and interactional factors related to request formats and the different understandings of ownership and entitlement that request formats reflect (Editorial, 2015: 3).

Rossi (2015) who explores the request format *hai x* in terms of sequence organization, argues that although the format *hai x* is used to ask if the requestee is in possession of the requested object, actually it is not used to make a request, rather a pre-request. Different from the format *hai x* treating the requested object as the possession of the requestee, *Can I have x* in Zinken's study (2015) treats the requested object as a shared good belonging to the requester and the requestee and as being in the requestee's control. The request made by *Can I have x* is the contingent outcome of ongoing courses of action (Zinken, 2015: 23). The format *Can I have x* displays the requester's high entitlement to the requested object and a strong expectation of compliance. Shared goods and the timing of the request format are two factors contributing to the expectation of the requester's compliance. An obligation emerging from the contingent control over a shared object makes the request grantable. At the right time when the requestee stops using the requested object, the requester makes a request, and also makes the request grantable.

Dixon (2015) compares the two request forms: the imperative construction "gimme" requests and grabbing gestures, both of which convey an expectation of compliance, and reveals that this expectation is related to ownership and entitlement. The last two works both contribute to the research on children's socialization. Instead of analyzing a request format, Takada and Endo (2015) explore the entire process of object transfer, which plays an important role in children's socialization. They identify that request-acceptance sequence in interaction between caregivers and children (aged 0-5 years) is closely related to the trigger of the object request, the features of the requested object and timing, bodily orientation, and the manner of transferring the requested object (Takada & Endo, 2015: 52) and show that culturally shared morality of Japan is constructed in object request sequences. By examining children's requests for food in Polish during mealtimes, Ogiermann (2015) shows that children's requests directed at their parents display not only a high entitlement but also an expectation of compliance, from the nature of requested object being free and parents' obligation to feed children. Ogiermann's findings are inconsistent with what has been found in previous research. Different request formats are classified into two categories: one is composed of direct and on-record requests, such as imperative, want statements and performatives; the other is conventionally indirect requests, such as interrogatives with modal verbs, rather than embodying different degrees of directness.

2.3.2.3 Interactional environments

Besides the afore-reviewed research concerning factors related to how request turns are designed in different formats, there are other elements such as interactional environments and speakers' contributions which are closely related to the production and formulations of requesting (Rossi, 2012; Taleghani-Nikazm, 2005 & 2006; Wootton, 1997 & 2005 and Zinken & Ogiermann, 2013). According to Wootton's study (1997) of request formats employed by children at the age of three, imperatives are used by the children in situations in which their requests are consistent with their parents' (namely, the requestee's) current line of action. The interrogative *Can you X?* is used when the child's request is perceived as potentially disruptive to the requestee's current course of activity. Rossi's findings (2012) are congruent with Wootton's. Imperatives are selected in the interactional environments where the requested action contributes to the established joint project involving requesters as well as requestees. The *Mi X?* format (a polar question in the second person in Italian), on the other hand, is selected when the requested action benefits the requester only. Requests formulated with imperatives and polar questions are named as unilateral requests and bilateral requests respectively. Zinken and Ogiermann's (2013) comparative study on imperatives and second-person polar questions used to make object requests in English and Polish family mealtimes identifies the home environments in which the two grammatical formats are used. Imperatives are selected in situations where requestees are involved in the wider project for co-owners; by contrast, second-person polar questions are used in situations in which requestees depart from their current trajectory of action. The actions implemented by imperatives and second-person polar questions are named as drawing on shared responsibility and enlisting assistance respectively. What Taleghani-Nikazm's (2005) findings demonstrate is another kind of interactional environment where contingent requests occur in the format of conditional *wenn*-clauses in German. The conditional *wenn*-clauses are a device for requesters to display their orientation to the contingent circumstances consequential from the extending of pre-request sequences.

2.3.2.4 Deontic authority

Deontic authority is about determining what "will be true" and as a logical consequence of that, what ought to be done (Stevanovic, 2011: 2). When it comes to deontic authority, Stevanovic puts forward two notions: deontic stance and deontic status. The former refers to the relative strength of deontic rights claimed by the choice of the form of the utterance, while the latter can be regarded as the deontic rights that a certain person has irrespective of whether she momentarily claims these right or not (Stevanovic, 2011: 4). From the perspective of deontic rights in action formation and taking declarative requests as an example, Stevanovic (2011) demonstrates how the two kinds of declarative statements concerning (1) the speaker and (2) future actions are deployed to make requests and are recognized as requests by participants. She argues that deontic rights are a decisive factor in action formation, by which requesters design their turns to implement requests and requestees interpret their co-participants' action as requests. It is the deontic status, rather than deontic stance, that plays a part in making declarative statements as requests from the part of requesters and recognizing those formats as requests from the part of requestees. Deontic rights, an important factor, together with agency are considered in the analysis of Couper-Kuhlen and Etelämäki (2015) who argue that requests and proposals belong to conversational directives. In their analysis of Finnish conversation, requests are considered actions with deontic asymmetry, which implies that speakers have strong rights to decide the future on the part of the directive speaker coupled with weaker rights on the part of recipient (Couper-Kuhlen & Etelämäki, 2015: 23). The strong deontic rights are displayed in expression of the speaker's request with certain necessity or desirability and nomination of the other as the agent who will do the request with explicit personal references. By contrast, the weaker deontic rights are displayed by zero-person constructions.

2.3.2.5 Studies on turn design of requesting from other perspectives

In this part, still other studies on designs of requesting turn from other perspectives will be reviewed.

From the relationship between grammar and action implemented by linguistic formats, Couper-Kuhlen (2014) proposes a taxonomy of directive-commissive actions including proposals, requests, offers and suggestions. According to her study, requests are a type of action that something will be done by the recipient at his or her cost and for the speaker's benefit. Drawing on her taxonomy, Clayman and Heritage (2014) make an analysis of requests and offers from the perspective of benefactive stance and status.

They propose that benefactive stance of requests is usually congruent with benefactive status, but when these two factors are incongruent, it is the benefactive status that plays a decisive role in the ascription of requesting. The selection of linguistic formats of the requesting turn is also influenced by multimodal resources in Sorjonen and Raevaara's study (2014). They concern the choice between a phrasal (NP) and a clausal format interplayed with bodily resources in launching and presenting requests for tobacco products at kiosks in Finland. They draw a conclusion that requests, treated as joint activities, are achieved at the counter and by participants' (namely both the sellers' and the customers') stationary position. The options for formats are related to the coordination among the arrangements of the physical space, the participants' location and bodily movement together with the sequential trajectory of the transaction. The selection of a clause format is employed to deal with the time spent by the customer to reach the counter, the transaction point, displaying the customer's orientation to the distance between her/him and the seller.

2.3.3 Requests and directives

The existing studies also investigate requests and directives from the perspective of the difference between the two actions (Craven & Potter, 2010) and the perspective of considering one as a constituent of the other (Goodwin & Cekaite, 2014).

Taking the concept of contingency from the study by Curl and Drew (2008), Craven and Potter (2010) differentiate requests from directives. As they termed that a directive is an action that speakers tell recipients to do something and a request is an action that speakers ask recipients to do something, directives embody high entitlement to direct recipients' action and no orientation to recipients' ability or willingness to perform the directed action, while requests embody lower entitlement to direct recipients' action. The difference between requests and directives is also revealed in terms of recipients' orientation, directives make compliance the relevant response, and even non-compliance to the first directive will lead to an up-graded directive, while requests make acceptance or refusal the relevant response.

Taking requests as one constituent of directives, Goodwin and Cekaite (2014) examine directives and response sequences with a specific concern of action formation, syntactic formats and prosody used to build directives and their responses, particularly the haptic forms used to get children to bed together with the bodily construction of directives and responses in English and Swedish family interactions. They not only demonstrate how interactants calibrate actions with respect to each other's action, but also present to us an indication that by the way of structuring directive trajectories, parents can be at the helm of stage form children's learning form of accountability and assist children in acquiring cooperative ways of being in the world.

2.3.4　Effects of reasons/accounts of requests

Reasons (or accounts) make requests understandable, increasing the likelihood of compliance (Davidson, 1984; Pomerantz, 1984; Wootton, 1981; Baranova and Dingemanse, 2016). However, besides this normal function, in existing studies reasons have other functions according to their sequential positions.

By a close examination of the sequential position, the content and the grammatical structure of accounts for requests in German, Taleghani-Nikazm (2006) argues that similar to English conversation, accounts are a design feature of requests and have two interactional functions according to their placements in request sequences. There are two placements for accounts – the "before-request-response" position and "after-request-acceptance" position, which function to pursue an acceptance from the recipient and as a "threat-and-conflict avoidance" (Heritage, 1984a) strategy to perform "remedial work" (Goffman, 1971) respectively. As for the content of accounts, it refers to some issues out of the requester's control or something unable to be got by the requester, which points to the "no fault" (Heritage, 1984a) quality of accounts for requests, serving to avoid threatening the recipient's face and co-participants' relationship. In addition to the position and content of accounts, the grammatical structure of accounts serves as affiliative moves. Accounts introduced by the causal connector *weil* display a marked word order by the placement of the finite verb in second position in the causal *weil*-clause. The early (second) positioning of the finite verb has dual functions: one is as a cohesive device facilitating the understanding of the account turn; the other is as resources for the projection of the upcoming talk and the action to be constructed. Taleghani-Nikazm suggests that it is the management of the relationship between co-participants and the maintenance of social solidarity (– the underlying structure of social interaction) that organizes the above three elements of accounts (Baranova & Dingemanse, 2016; Taleghani-Nikazm, 2006, etc.).

By contrasting request sequences with and without reasons, Baranova and Dingemanse (2016) find that in Russian reasons may be implicit and explicit and are mainly encountered in four sequential positions, which is a piece of evidence for participants' orientation to the need for a reason. And by the four sequential positions, (namely being positioned (1) after the absence of immediate compliance, (2) together with requests, (3) as pre-requests and (4) after compliance or acceptance), reasons deal with three issues – providing information for the underspecified requests, managing relationship potentially damaged by delicacy of requests and offering explanation of ancillary action implemented by requests.

2.3.5 Recruitment of assistance

Drew and Couper-Kuhlen (2014) make an analysis of requesting in a broader sense of recruitments, which is interpreted as a specific kind of requests, both a narrower and a broader notion than that of requests in terms of the requested object or action, precondition for achievement of requests and ways to initiation of requests respectively. They focus on the visual and nonverbal dimensions in requests ignored in traditional analyses, describe the beauty of recruitments and conditions for achieving them, identify remedial procedures subsequent to unsuccessful uptake of recruitment displays, and clarify relation of recruitments to offers, all of which provide us insight into future investigations.

Kendrick and Drew (2016) further examine requests under the umbrella of recruitment, which covers the linguistic and embodied ways not only to request or solicit assistance, but also to offer assistance when we perceive other's need and which refers to an interactional outcome or effect achieved by different methods in interaction. They hold that recruitments and subsidiary action are constituents of cooperation in social life and the cooperative and altruistic character of recruitments is the foundation of maintenance of social cohesion at the micro level of social life. Requests coupled with the other four alternative methods – reports, alerts, embodied displays and projections/anticipations are used by participants for recruitment in the face of troubles in progressing a course of action in ordinary face-to-face interaction. The five methods form a continuum, ranging from the most explicit request, to less ones including the verbal report or display of difficulties and embodied display of difficulties, by which the requester can solicit an offer, and to those the most implicit ones in which the other preempts an offer to obviate the anticipatory troubles without elicitation of assistance. The differences of these methods lie in three aspects: ways of recognizing troubles, the relevance of assistance as a response, the person who initiates the recruitment of assistance in different sequence organization and the person who provides a possible resolution and the provided solutions as offers of assistance or provisions of assistance. Besides, they identify a kind of novel action preceding recruitments named as subsidiary action, functioning to display difficulties and providing opportunities for others to assist.

As a complementary to the work by Kendrick and Drew (2016), Zinken and Rossi (2016) argue that in order to have a better understanding of assistance and contribution, it is necessary to examine demonstrable commitments and responsibilities that participants to interaction have to one another (Zinken & Rossi, 2016: 21). There are other forms of cooperative engagement which can be served as recruitment in interaction, such as imperative requests, which is omitted by Kendrick and Drew, established commitments, which is the base for non-verbally recruitment and assistance demonstrably oriented to established commitments.

2.3.6 Studies on requesting from other perspectives

There are studies on requesting from other perspectives, such as practices for division-of-labor proposals in requests in English and Finnish (Couper-Kuhlen & Etelämäki, 2014), practices for requesting functioning to demonstrate that a request is endogenously treated by both the requester and the requestee as a face-threatening act as well as a dispreferred initiative action (Yu Guodong, 2019), requesting as a vehicle for other actions (Mandelbaum, 2014), multimodal resources deployed for requesting as embodied action in the institutional setting (Mondada, 2014), contrastive study on behavioral designs in requests and offers between orangutans and human infants (Rossano & Liebal, 2014), to name but only a few.

2.4 Requests in Other Fields

Given the limited space, requests in other fields such as sociolinguistics, cognitive linguistics and second language acquisition will be briefly summarized. In sociolinguistics, attention is paid to the influence of different social variables on realization of request strategies, such as Pan Yulin (1994) and Wang Xiaotong (2012), etc. Pan (1994) makes an analysis of speech acts in terms of politeness strategies in Chinese in official, business and family settings. He holds that when the speech activity takes place (e.g. request) different social factors such as age, gender, official rank and in-group identity play a different role in the selection of politeness strategies according to different settings. In the official setting, superior-subordinate hierarchy is resorted to. In the seller-buyer business setting, the relationship between the seller and the buyer determines what type of strategies is used in the interaction. When it is recognized as an outside relation, the bald-on-record strategy is used, while if it is as an inside one, the selected strategy display this kind of relationship and camaraderie. An inside relation can also be created by applying strategies to show politeness. And in the family setting, especially in a dinner-table conversation, position in the hierarchical system of the family is the decisive factor in the choice of strategies. Wang (2012) examines the influence of the five social variables (including social power, social distance, age, rank of imposition and gender) on the performance of request in Chinese. The former three exert a stronger influence than the latter two on the selection of request strategies. The more power the speaker has, the more direct the strategy is used. The closer the distance between the speaker and the recipient, the more direct the strategy is used. If it is made by younger speakers to older hearers, the request is more direct, more heavily and politely modified and with more either 1 alerter or >1 alerter.

CHAPTER TWO LITERATURE REVIEW

Contrarily, if it is made by older speakers to younger hearers, the request is more indirect, less modified internally and with noticeably less alerters.

Cognitive linguistics focuses on the deep structures of requests and request strategies, and re-interpretation of requests with different theories in this field, say, the Conceptual Blending Theory. Based on Panther and Thornburg's speech act scenario and Mendoza and Hernandez's cognitive description of the request speech act, Ju Zhiqin (2007) re-classifies request structures into four types: opting out; structure core; structure core + branches, (which is most frequently explored in Chinese) and structure branches. He also points out that the speaker's selection of request structures and strategies can be influenced by social distance, relative power and the nature of request. Jia Shaomin's study (2011) provides a meaning construction mechanism – conceptual blending theory together with metonymy by which indirect speech acts (e.g. request) can be comprehensively explained and interpreted. It is with the help of this powerful mechanism that people can understand meaning of indirect speech acts fast.

And in second language acquisition, scholars aim to offer some implications for teaching and learning a second language by investigations of requests on the basis of the second language acquisition approach (Yang Xianju, 2006; Liu Chenyan, 2014; etc.). Focusing on the acquisition-phase of the speech act of requests in English, Yang (2006) and Liu (2014) respectively study the pragmatic development and the pragmatic competence of second language learners at different proficiency levels in Chinese and English. Yang points out that the acquisition of pragmatic competence is influenced by two more factors – L1 pragmatic transfer and classroom instructions, besides the effect of L2 proficiency. Liu argues that teachers should help learners overcome negative transfer of the mother tongue and improve learners' available pragmatic input. They both stress the importance of L1 pragmatic transfer and pragmatic input in second language teaching and learning.

2.5 Delicacy

The idea of studying delicacy can be traced back to the traditional ways to give explanation for people's behavior when sensitivity is at stake: one focuses on individual cognitions, while the other emphasizes effects of cultural rules and values on the social value of certain issues and how people solves these issues in public and private environments. Despite cultural values or personal features, interaction, in symbolic interactionist theories, is taken into account in explaining sensitivity (van Nijnatten & Suoninen, 2014). This idea is supported by Goffman (1959) who treats social interaction as a dramaturgical performance, in which people involve in impression management and deal with social relations by preserving face for both others and themselves. Following Goffman's works, most of this literature has been concerned with that adequate understanding of human activities which are dynamic should be extended in and through interactions with co-participants (Drew & Heritage, 1992; Garfinkel, 1967; Sacks, 1992; Silverman, 1997). In line with the literature, delicacy is studied as locally produced interactional phenomenon (Bergmann, 1992; Linell & Bredmar, 1996; Silverman, 1987 & 1997; Silverman & Peräkylä, 1990; van Nijnatten & Suoninen, 2014; Weijts, Houtkoop & Mullen, 1993; Yu & Wu, 2015, etc.). Studies on the management of delicacy are mainly investigated in institutional interactions, such as medical encounters and interviews, etc. from two perspectives: sequentiality and turn designs.

In terms of sequentiality, delay, a favorite way achieved through different devices is frequently employed to mark potentially delicate matters. The perspective-display series is a useful practice used by clinicians when they are in the process of a delivery of bad diagnosis. It not only delays the occurrence of the diagnosis but also facilitates patients' understanding of what may be referred to by the clinical terms related to the diagnosis and upgrades, as for patients, the possibility of acceptance of the diagnosis (Maynard, 1991). In Yu and Wu's study, two kinds of delay are observed. First, the turn where the word *nage* (which refers to sex organs or sex-related problems) exists is sequentially delayed. Second, a delay in using *nage* itself or using *nage* to delay mentioning the sex organ or sex-related problems is identified. Delaying the reference to mention the sex organ or sex-related problems by *nage* in Chinese functions to distance the caller himself from the mentioned sex-related topics (Yu & Wu, 2015). Delay is also found in other researchers' works, such as Suoninen (1999), Weijts et al. (1993), to name but only a few.

As is shown in the literature, the major turn maneuvers deployed to mark delicacy are expressive of caution and discretion represented by delays, downgrades, perturbations, avoidance, mitigation, depersonalization and indirectness, etc. and elaborations and story prefaces. Analyzing psychiatric intake interview, Bergmann (1992) finds many forms of expressive caution such as softening words foreshadowing upcoming potentially delicate matters and litotes, namely assertions denying the opposite of what is being indicated, inviting the interviewee to identify an unspecified issue by offering information and impressions. In addition to expressive caution (e.g. delay of the delicate matter and various perturbations), Silverman (1997) finds that both HIV counselors and clients use elaborations and story prefaces to express potentially delicate issues. In interactions counselors usually use devices like perspective-display sequences, justifications and indirect questions, etc. to create a favorable environment for clients to provide delicate information, while clients also invoke membership categorization devices which carry strong implications about category-bound activities to mark potentially delicate items and simultaneously make them excusable and reasonable. Based on the detailed analysis, Silverman suggests that the management of delicacy seemingly is a cooperative matter between counselors and clients. Linell and Bredmar

(1996) investigate how three potentially delicate topics are managed in a primary health care unit through indirectness and mitigation between newly pregnant women and midwives. Because of the different nature of those three topics – smoking and drinking, the syphilis and HIV and the fetal anomalies and possible abortion (Linell & Bredmar, 1996: 370), there are still other distinctive ways to deal with them respectively. The treatment of the topic about smoking and drinking is characterized by introducing an immediate way and using mitigation and a limited depth of penetration, whereas that of topics about syphilis and HIV is featured by a reframing and a delayed way. Topics about fetal anomalies and possible abortion are dealt with in the same way as the syphilis and HIV topics. Weijts, Houtkoop and Mullen (1993) analyze how physicians and patients coopertatively accomplish potentially delicate issues by expressive caution in gynaecological consultations. Expressive caution can be marked by delays, avoidances and depersonalizations. Their findings provide useful insight in medical practices. By analyzing the use of *nage* in radio phone-in medical consultations in Chinese, Yu and Wu (2015) identify that *nage* functions as a delicate issue managing practice either in the stand-alone form or in the compounded form "*nage* + noun". The dual interactional imports of *nage* are to distance the caller herself/himself from the sex-related topics involved and to build himself as a victim of the sex-related problems as well. Van Nijnatten and Suoninen (2015) focus on how social workers and their clients mark topics as delicate, which is termed as doing delicacy. By doing delicacy social workers create a positive atmosphere in terms of maintaining harmonious, continuous and smooth conversation. That is, in such atmosphere it is easy not only for social workers to give personal advice and hint, but also for clients to disclose potentially delicate information.

The existing delicacy-related studies mainly involve institutional interactions. Due to the asymmetry of the institutional identity, deontic and epistemic status between the speaker and the hearer, the social actions implemented in these institutional settings are colored with delicate features. The current issue is whether social actions, such as requesting, conducted in mundane settings, also display the feature of delicacy. If it is so, are the practices of doing delicacy in mundane settings similar to or different from those employed in institutional settings? This is the major research question of the present study.

2.6　Comments on the Existing Studies

Based on the afore-mentioned review, it is apparent that studies on requesting in diverse disciplines are different in respect of their focuses because of different research methodologies. While the speech act theory explores the felicity conditions which defines a speech act as a request, the politeness-related studies focuses on the degrees of politeness when the various ways of requesting are considered in terms of imposition, social distance, deference and other social variables. The cross-cultural pragmatics makes contrastive studies on request strategies of eight languages, and sociolinguistics mainly studies influences exerted on the speaker's choice of request strategies by different social variables like age, gender and rank, etc. The above-mentioned approaches to requesting have provided the academia a comprehensive understanding about requesting, a ubiquitous social action of human beings. But still some limitations in the existing studies need to be resolved in future studies. The speech-act oriented studies usually use single utterances as their data without taking the context into consideration. Invented or fabricated data have also been used in traditional linguistic research and politeness-related or strategy-related research. Questionnaires and interviews etc. have also been major sources of non-natural data in the previous studies. Social actions like requesting are sensitive to both sequential context and social context. Therefore, the data collected in non-natural settings or the fabricated data have overlooked the context-sensitive nature of social actions.

However, focusing on actual details of actual actions of social life, conversation analysis aims to examine how people achieve whatever they do achieve and discover the machinery concealed in social interaction. As a result, naturally occurring data are typically required. Studies on request in this field have mainly investigated how a series of different syntactic formats are used to get request fulfilled, and have explained how and why different grammatical formats are identifiable as requests, and have concerned the designs of responses to requests and request sequences, etc. Works such as Curl and Drew (2008), Wootton (1981, 1997 & 2005) and Rossi (2012) have shown that selections of linguistic formats cannot be explained only in terms of variables such as the age or gender of requestees or impositions on requestees. This is because there are cases in which grammatical formats used to perform a request are different when the above-mentioned variables are constant. The research methodology of conversation analysis is more comprehensive and accurate in analyzing how and why requesting is implemented by diverse grammatical formats at a particular position and at a particular time.

Employing naturally occurring conversation as its data and conversation analysis as its methodology, the present study investigates how requesting is treated as being delicate in terms of sequence organization and turn design in Mandarin Chinese.

2.7 Summary

In this chapter, the previous studies on requesting have been reviewed, covering pragmatics, sociolinguistics, and conversation analysis, etc. Based on this review, findings of the existing studies are displayed, and research questions are presented as well. The research methodology of conversation analysis will be introduced in the next chapter before we extend the main body of this study.

CHAPTER THREE   RESEARCH METHODOLOGY

   The present study employs Conversation Analysis as its research methodology. Conversation Analysis (hereafter CA) with its origins in sociology can be traced back to the 1960s' America. Methodologically, CA tries to expose, describe and explicate practices or methods through which social members produce and interpret social actions. The aim of this chapter is to make a brief introduction to the origin and theoretical background, development and classification, scientificity and basic notions of CA as a research methodology and the research procedures of this study.

3.1   Origins and Development of CA

   CA was developed by Harvey Sacks, the founder, together with Emanuel A. Schegloff and Gail Jefferson in the late 1960s. Dissenting from the view that conversation in everyday life is chaotic and disorderly, and is of no value to research, CA draws inspiration from two great sociologists – Erving Goffman and Harold Garfinkel.

3.1.1   Influence of Erving Goffman

   Goffman (1983) argues that social interaction is highly organized and inherently ordered, and embodies a distinct institutional order, in his terms "the interaction order". This interaction order which should be studied in its own right is a kind of moral order comprised of a set of normative rights and obligations which regulate interaction and have a linkage to "face", other features of identity and macro social institutions. Moreover, interaction order with its own social institution is the basis for other social institutions, such as hospitals, educations and courts of law, etc. According to Goffman, there is in such an order an underlying structure organization, namely syntax, by which he means that "the proper study of interaction is not the individual and his psychology, but rather the syntactical relations among the acts of different persons mutually present to one another" (Goffman, 1967: 2). As a central part of the moral order, the syntax of interaction provides a criterion of judgment for personal conduct, motivations and identities. It is the place where face, self, and identity are expressed, and where they are also ratified or undermined by the conduct of others (Heritage & Clayman, 2010: 9). In a word, what Goffman is interested in is how face and identity are associated with action, and how moral inferences about them can motivate interactional conduct (Heritage & Clayman, 2010: 9). Although inspiration emanated from Goffman is influential, it does not touch upon the question that how mutual understanding of participants during the process of interaction is achieved and how it propels interaction. What is neglected by Goffman is right what Garfinkel is concerned about. What follows is a brief description about Garfinkel's influence on CA.

3.1.2 Influence of Harold Garfinkel

Under the influence of phenomenology of Alfred Schutz and Edmund Husserl, and rather than taking social order as a result of socialization and the internalization of norms, Garfinkel proposes ethnomethodology which is a "bottom-up" method to investigate social actions in everyday life. He argues that it is the shared practical reasoning and common sense knowledge that lay a solid foundation for social life. To test his ideas, Garfinkel uses the "breach experiments", that is, to breach taken-for-granted background expectancies. For instance, students in one experiment are demanded to spend from fifteen minutes to an hour in their homes imagining that they were boarders and acting out this assumption. They were instructed to conduct themselves in circumspect and polite fashion. They were to avoid getting personal, to use formal address, to speak only when spoken to (Garfinkel, 1967: 47). According to the report of student experimenters, Garfinkel finds that confusion and indignation are engendered among the family members when they could not figure out the situation. And they usually would make sense of the strange actions and make the situation restore normal appearance. As in Garfinkel's words, the activities whereby members produce and manage the settings of organized everyday affairs are identical with members' procedures for making these settings accountable (Garfinkel, 1967: 1). In other words, methods that participants use to produce action are the same as methods that participants use to recognize and understand them.

In a word, from Goffman, CA absorbs the idea that social interaction constituting its own organization orderly named as interaction order which could be studied in its own institution. From Garfinkel, what CA draws is the underlying effects of the shared practical reasoning in action's production, recognition and understanding in social interaction (Heritage & Clayman, 2010).

3.1.3 Development and classification of CA

According to Stivers and Sidnell (2013) the development course of CA can be divided into four periods – the rudimentary stage, the burgeoning stage, the growth stage and the mature stage.

From its inception (since 1967), CA has developed into a special research style of its own. Inspired by the two seminal thinkers Goffman and Garfinkel, Harvey Sacks (1935-1975), the founder of CA, accepted the invitation from Garfinkel in 1963 to be engaged in a program of the Suicide Prevention Center at UCLA. It is this work that paves the way for the emergence of CA as a discipline of its own (Schegloff, in Sacks, 1992a). Based on the suicide calls recorded by the center, Sacks noted that a device ("This is Mr. Smith may I help you") was used by the call-takers to get the callers' names without asking for it. And with "I can't hear you" the callers initiating a repair could avoid giving their names as a relevant response. Moreover, he also investigated the way of producing the accounts of their troubles used by the callers, which was a critical step toward the exploration of conversational turn taking, sequential structures or patterns as well as management of activities in conversation (Lerner, 2004).

In his earlier work, Sacks' interest was in membership categorization analysis and sequential analysis. In the observation of recordings of suicide calls, Sacks noted that in conversation person-categories as part of sets of categories were often used, which was termed "Membership Categorization Devices" (MCDs; Sacks, 1972a; 1972b). Categories are not just named or implied, they also carry a number of different associated properties, later called category predicates, like the one that Sacks used a lot: category-bound activities (ten Have, 2007: 47). After around 1967, Sacks paid more attention to sequential analysis, which is the focus of the current CA works.

The papers such as *Sequencing in conversational openings* written by Schegloff (1968), *Opening up closings* co-written by Schegloff and Sacks (1973) and *A simplest systematics for the organization of turn-taking for conversation* co-written by Sacks, Schegloff and Jefferson (1974) also played an important role in promoting the development of CA. Besides, the system of transcription developed by Gail Jefferson was a great contribution to CA, which has been used by conversation analysts ever since. Although the data used by Sacks and Schegloff were recorded in institutional settings from suicide calls and tape-recorded group therapy sessions, and a disaster center respectively, their papers mainly focused on basic issues in ordinary conversations instead of institutional ones. From the late 1970s on, CA researchers turned their attention to institutional interactions such as emergency calls, clinic conversation, courtroom conversation and different sorts of interviews. Their focus was how conversations were processed differently in different institutional settings and how institutional interactions come into being (ten Have, 2007). Due to shifted focus of CA research, CA has been classified into two types: pure CA and applied CA.

> There are, therefore, at least two kinds of conversation analytic research going on today, and, though they overlap in various ways, they are distinct in focus. The first examines the institution of interaction as an entity in its own right; the second studies the management of social institutions in interaction.
>
> (Heritage, 1997: 162)

The former is what is called as pure CA and the latter applied CA. CA was originally developed as a "pure" science, motivated by the wish to discover basic and general aspects of sociality (ten Have, 2007: 174). Most of the early studies in CA centered on ordinary conversations, which means that settings of conversations are not confined to any specialized contexts or to any particular activities. The focus on institutional talks, which involve particular goals of the participants and special constraints on environments began in the late 1970s. Both studies on ordinary conversations and institutional talks belong to the type of pure CA, whereas applied CA has come to denote the possibilities of using CA to elucidate of practical situations and efforts to make social life better in some way (ten Have, 2007: 174, 194).

CA breasted the waves in 1980s a burgeoning stage despite the difficulty due to the tragic death of Harvey Sacks in 1975. A number of conversation analysts made great contributions during this decade. They not only engaged in research and training students, such as Gail Jefferson and Anita Pomerantz but also published lots of important articles, such as Charles Goodwin, John Heritage whose *Garfinkel and Ethnomethodology* (1984) not merely give an exegesis of the roots of Garfinkel's thinking but also a classic introduction of CA from a sociological perspective (Stivers & Sidnell, 2013: 4), to name but a few. Some significant works of them deserve to be mentioned, such as Atkinson and Heritage's (1984) *Structures of Social Action: Studies in Conversation Analysis* which presents a collection of what remain some of the most cited papers in CA, Paul Drew and Anthony Wootton's (1987) *Erving Goffman: Exploring the Interaction Order* which includes important contributions on Goffman's relation to CA by Schegloff and Heath, and Button and Lee's (1987) *Talk and Social Organization* which contains a series of important studies by Sacks, Schegloff, Jefferson, Goodwin and others, etc. (Stivers & Sidnell, 2013: 4-5).

The 1990s witnessed a vigorous growth of CA, during which more and more CA researchers got permanent positions at universities, which led to more and more courses towards CA. Moreover, it was propulsion to establish centers of CA scholarship and training at UCLA, UCSB, the University of York and the University of Helsinki. The booming discussions about CA as a widely recognized method across different conferences under different disciplines such as linguistic anthropology, pragmatics, discursive psychology and ethnomethodology, etc. undoubtedly contributed to the prosperity of CA in the world (Stivers & Sidnell, 2013).

CHAPTER THREE RESEARCH METHODOLOGY

Since 2000, CA has witnessed a mature stage with steady increases in CA scholarship. The first International Conference on Conversation Analysis held in Copenhagen in 2002 representing a milestone in CA history. And the second in Helsinki in 2006, the third in Mannheim in 2010, the fourth at UCLA in 2014, and the fifth in the UK in 2018 were also epoch-making. In a word, CA has been an influential methodology across different disciplines.

3.2 The Scientificity of CA

Different from quantitative research which needs more data and the more, the better, CA does not have a prescribed amount of data, as Sacks maintains that the detailed study of small phenomena may give an enormous understanding of the way humans to things and the kinds of objects they use to construct and order their affairs (Jefferson, 1985: 26). As a qualitative research method, the scientificity of CA is embodied in the following essential properties.

3.2.1 Naturally occurring data

One of the basic requirements in CA is that the analyzed data must be recordings of naturally occurring interaction. The so-called "naturally occurring" means that conversations are collected by audio or video recordings from real ordinary life or institution talk without any preconceptions of who the participants are, how to communicate with each other or what kinds of conversation will be got. In addition to the fact that recordings of natural data are the basis of the fulfillment of CA's goal which not only describes the practices in human interaction but also uncovers and elucidates the underlying organization in everyday life, there are several advantages to use the naturally occurring recordings of interactions.

The benefit of using actual recordings is to avoid (1) suspicion that people do not talk in such a manner which is a phenomenon in the invented or imagined data (Sacks, 1984); (2) memory limitations of observers by field notes; (3) external interference with the naturalness of conversation by interviews, questionnaires or experiments and (4) nonequivalence by introspection (Mondada, 2013; ten Have, 2007). Although for CA, interviews are a situated practice characteristic of certain professions, which can be studied to reveal how these practitioners work, it cannot used as a methodology for gathering data (Mondada, 2013: 33). There is another merit to use actual recordings, namely, not only to enable the conversation analysts study the recorded materials again and again, but also to offer readers or other people who disagree with researchers opportunities to study the recorded interaction in the same way as researchers do (ten Have, 2007).

3.2.2　The system of transcription

When doing conversation analysis, conversation analysts do not merely listen carefully to recordings, they also rely on the transcript which is a necessary auxiliary for analysis in a meticulous way. The work of transcriptions is made following the transcription system invented by Gail Jefferson (1984) to represent the original interaction, with a requirement that not only what is said but also how is said should be included in transcripts (ten Have, 2007). Conversation analysts have to train themselves to listen carefully enough to be fully aware of subtle nuances of the talk-in-interaction. Although it is a time-consuming work, the process of transcribing helps conversation analysts to notice and understand particular phenomenon, events or participants' actions (Heath & Luff, 1993), for only by repeated listening or viewing can the detailed transcript be obtained. And transcripts whose accuracy will be

CHAPTER THREE RESEARCH METHODOLOGY

maintained by data session (which will be discussed in section 3.2.5) also make readers or audiences accessible to the phenomenon or action being studied, for transcripts are required to have equal effects with listening to audio recordings as detailed as possible.

3.2.3 A quasi-natural scientific approach

CA is more of natural sciences than social sciences from the perspective of its ways of doing research. The first step to start the analysis of CA is observation – treating the recorded materials at hand as specimen and unmotivated looking[①] at them to find patterns or regularities and to explicate their logic as the natural scientists make close looking at their specimen, rather than from any preconceived ideas or common sense presuppositions (Hutchby & Wooffitt, 1998; Sidnell, 2010; ten Have, 2007). As Psathas writes:

> The variety of interactional phenomena available for study are not selected on the basis of some preformulated theorizing, which may specify matters of greater or lesser significance. Rather the first stages of research have been characterized as unmotivated looking. Data may be obtained from any available source, the only requirements being that these should be naturally occurring.
>
> (Psathsa, 1995: 45)

[①] This [unmotivated looking] is, of course, a contradiction or paradox since looking is motivated or there would be no looking being done in the first place. It is a term which is intended to imply that the investigator is "open" to discovering phenomena rather than searching for instances of already identified and described phenomena or for some theoretically preformulated conceptualization of what the phenomena should look like (Psathas, 1990: 24-5, n.3).

As a method with stricture, CA does not deny the fact that there are differences between persons with regard to power, status and so on. It does not suppose that these differences are a necessary predetermined factor in the production of a particular episode of talk or other activities. They may be consequential, and in terms of CA, their functions should be demonstrated in the talk rather than assumed by the analysts (Sidnell, 2013). It is important to clarify that the deviant case analysis is an essential part of CA as an inductive method. It is necessary to analyze departures of some sort from a previously formulated pattern to explicate standard ones.

3.2.4 Contrastive analysis

The nature of CA is a contrastive study, which means that the process of analysis is permeated with comparisons, whatever comparisons are. There are comparisons between different alternative patterns or practices, comparisons between the routine and the deviant case within a class named as within-type comparisons and comparisons between informal or ordinary conversation and formal or institutional ones called as across-type comparisons (ten Have, 2007). Comparisons even can be made between different nations, cultures, and languages. For instance, the first three examples quoted in Sacks' first lecture are discussed in a comparative way, in which the first two are routine ways while the third one is a deviant instance that departs from the routine ones. A similar fashion is also used in Schegloff's analysis of conversational openings. It is the contrast between the routine and the deviant that does the trick here. It is used to open up the field for analysis. By comparing instances with each other, and with general experiences and expectations, their formatted properties, sequential placement, and local functionality can be related and explicated (ten Have, 2007: 24).

CHAPTER THREE   RESEARCH METHODOLOGY

3.2.5 Data session

It is the data session that is a unique feature of doing CA playing an important part in actual CA practice. A "data session" is an informal get-together of researchers in order to discuss some "data" – recordings and transcripts. The group may consist of a more or less permanent team of people working together on a project or in related projects, or an ad hoc meeting of independent researchers (ten Have, 2007: 140). The first step in the procedure for "doing" a data session is to bring in the data and transcripts by one member, followed by play recording of the data. Then some minutes are allotted to observe the data, preceded by the introduction of some background information by the provider of the data. After that the present members are required to present their observation about the data, and to deliver their points of view and confusion on any part that they are interested in. Then others can raise doubts and provide their distinct opinions or whatever concerning the speech of the previous participant (ten Have, 2007). Such a data session is very helpful and beneficial for every participant. First of all, under the collaborative observation, accuracy and objectivity of the transcript of the data is guaranteed. Secondly, in discussions the owner of the data could get a sort of mixture of diverse viewpoints, observations and practical or theoretical points, all of which would function as a motor to propel the development of the existing understanding or analysis. Moreover, collaborative viewing is particularly powerful for neutralizing preconceived notions on the part of researchers and discourages the tendency to see in the interaction what one is conditioned to see or even wants to see (Jordan & Henderson, 1995: 44). Last but not least, neophytes can make brilliant progress with more experienced CA analysts.

3.3 Basic Notions of CA

It is essential to make a sketch of some basic notions or tools of CA, before we do the following research. Since the foci of the present study are delicacy in requesting, multiple syntactic formats of requesting and reasons of different choices, basic notions – ranging from turn-taking, sequence organization, preference organization to turn design are introduced with no reference to repair due to its little-involvement in this investigation.

3.3.1 Turn taking system

A basic notion in CA is that a turn is a basic unit of conversation. A turn generally is a period of time during which one single participant speaks. According to Sacks, the most obvious feature of conversation is that people talk in turns. There is one single person talking at a time occasionally with minimal gaps or overlaps, which relies on the turn-taking system (Sacks, Scheloff & Jefferson, 1974). Turn-taking system is locally managed, party-administered, interactionally controlled and sensitive to recipient design, as characterized by Sacks, Schegloff and Jefferson. It is locally managed since it organizes only current and next turn and not, for instance, what will happen in thirty seconds, in five minutes or tomorrow. It is party-administered in the sense that there is no "referee" to determine who should speak next and for how long (Sidnell, 2010: 39). It is interactionally controlled since any feature is multilaterally shaped and recipient design refers to a multitude of respects in which talk by a party in a conversation is constructed or designed in ways which display an orientation and sensitivity to the particular other(s) who are the co-participants (Sacks, Schegloff & Jefferson, 1974: 727). In other words, turn-taking system is machinery of interesting properties. It is

CHAPTER THREE RESEARCH METHODOLOGY

locally sensitive and is fine-tuned to certain recipients, functioning as a processor to make the parties as participants in conversation. In order to get a comprehensive understanding of turn-taking system, it is necessary to begin with Turn Constructional Unit (shortened as TCU) and Transition Relevant Place (shortened as TRP).

TCU is the building block of a turn that consists of one TCU or multi-TCUs. The shape of TCUs can be sentences, clauses, phrases or words. And it can also be non-lexical items such as "huh?". In conversations, the capacity of TCU – projectability – makes it possible that participants could project different types of TCUs and the possible completion of the current turn according to grammar, intonation and action. When there is a possible completion of a turn, there is Transition Relevant Place (shortened as TRP). TRP is a place where a possibility for turn transition is provided but transition of turns will likely but not certainly happen. When it happens, transition of turns is directed by the following rules:

Rule 1 – applies initially at the first TRP of any turn (C = current speaker, N = next speaker)

a If C selects N in current turn, then C must stop speaking, and N must speak next, transition occurring at the first possible completion after N-selection.

b If C does not select N, then any (other) party may self-select, first speaker gaining rights to the next turn,

c If C does not select N, and no other party self-selects under option (b), then C may (but need not) continue (i.e. claim rights to a further TCU).

Rule 2 – applies at all subsequent TRPs.

When Rule 1 (c) has been applied by C, then at the next TRP Rules 1 (a)- (c) apply, and recursively at the next TRP, until speaker change is effected (Sacks, Scheloff & Jefferson, 1974: 704).

3.3.2 Sequence organization

A second basic notion in CA is that conversation is sequentially organized. The idea of sequences refers to courses of action implemented through talk (Schegloff, 2007: 3). In CA enterprise, what are focused on is what kinds of actions are being implemented through talk; are there any patterns or practices can be isolated or described; are there any other practices or structures can serve as the vehicle for the same action; what came before the action – how the action is performed as a response to the previous one or as an initiative action and what will come after – what kinds of responses it will get in the next turn. So it is necessary to study sequence organization to explore the above issues about interactions in terms of the concept of Adjacency Pair (shortened as AP) which is more generally the basic unit of sequence organization (Schegloff, 2007).

3.3.2.1 Adjacency Pair

The notion of AP results from the study of "nextness" which means that what an utterance of a speaker not only has something to do with the previous utterances, but also puts some constraints on the subsequent utterances (Sacks, 1992a; Schegloff, 1968 & 2007; Stivers, 2013). This kind of "nextness" between neighboring utterances in conversations could be understood as "conditional relevance" in Schegloff's phrase: by the conditional relevance of one item on another we mean: given the first, the second is expectable; upon its occurrence it can be seen to be a second item to the first; upon its non-occurrence it can be seen to be officially absent – all this provided by the occurrence of the first item (Schegloff, 1968: 1083). As Sacks and Schegloff defined it, the twin turns belonging to different speakers with this kind of conditional relevance are AP, which has five features as follows: (1) AP is a minimal sequence composed of two

CHAPTER THREE RESEARCH METHODOLOGY

turns; (2) these two turns are produced by different speakers; (3) these two turns are adjacently placed; (4) these two turns are orderly organized as a first pair part (shortened as FPP) and a second pair part (shortened as SPP) and (5) these two turns are pair-type related; that is, a particular type of FPP is paired with a corresponding SPP (such as greeting – greeting, invitation – acceptance/rejection, assessment – agreement/disagreement, etc.). As a basic sequence, an AP could be, but need certainly not be expanded.

3.3.2.2 Sequence expansion

Sequence expansion which is not simply the extension of turns of an AP, can be positioned in three places – preceding, inserting or following an AP, which are named pre-expansion, insert expansion, and post-expansion respectively. It can be outlined as follows:

$$\text{base pair}\begin{cases}\text{First pair part}\\ \\ \text{Second pair part}\end{cases}\quad\begin{matrix}\leftarrow\text{pre-expansion}\\ \\ \leftarrow\text{insert expansion}\\ \\ \leftarrow\text{post expansion}\end{matrix}$$

(Sidnell, 2010: 95)

(1) Pre-expansion

Pre-expansion refers to sequence expansion occurring before the FPP of a base pair. Since the pre-expansion itself consists of APs, it could also be named pre-sequence (Sacks, 1992a). There are two kinds of pre-sequences – type-specific pre-sequence and generic pre-sequence. The former aims to project a specific base FPP, such as pre-invitation ("What are you going to do after work?") or pre-request ("Are you busy now, Lisa?") and to avoid occurrence of a negative base SPP. The latter however does not project any specific base FPP; rather it aims to guarantee recipiency – to attract attention of a projected recipient or to check the precondition of a projected conversation, such as summons-answer sequence. In addition, the pre-pre is a different kind of type-specific pre-sequence, taking the form of "Can I X" or "Let me X", in which "X" refers to a projected future action. Followed by "go-ahead" SPP, the pre-pre is not followed by the base FPP, rather a preliminary to the anticipated action by X. There are two kinds of preliminaries — pre-mentions and pre-conditions. The former involves a mention or provides background information related to the base FPP, but presumed to be unknown to the recipient; the latter involves establishment of pre-condition on which the propriety of the base FPP is contingent. Here are three examples showing these pre-sequences:

Ex. 1 (Cited from Drew, 2013b: 146)

```
01  Les:    Leslie he:re,
02  Car:    Ye(h)es,
03          (0.2)
04  Les:    .hhh U[hm
05  Car:          [Got the message,
06  Les:    Are you going t'night.
```

Ex. 2 (Cited from Schegloff, 2007: 30)

```
01  Cla:    Hello
02  Nel:    Hi.
03  Cla:    Hi.
04  Nel:    Whatcha doin'.
05  Cla:    Not much
06  Nel:    Y'wanna drink?
07  Cla:    Okay.
```

Ex. 3 (Cited from Schegloff, 2007: 45)

```
01  Fre:    Oh by the way ((sniff)) I have a bi:g
02          favor to ask ya.
03  Lau:    Sure, go'head.
04  Fre:    'Member the blouse you made a
```

CHAPTER THREE   RESEARCH METHODOLOGY

```
05          couple weeks ago?
06   Lau:   Ya.
07   Fre:   Well I want to wear it this weekend
08          to Vegas but my mom's buttonholer
09          is broken.
10   Lau:   Fred I told ya when I made the blouse I'd do
11          the buttonholes.
```

In Ex. 1, Les' self-identification in Line 01 and Car's answer in Line 02 are what is called generic pre-sequence, by which Les secures Car's attention and can carry on her talk overlapping with Car's. In Ex. 2, Line 01 and the untranscribed telephone ring are also a generic summons-answer pre-sequence. Lines 02-03 is greeting, by which self-identification and recognition are achieved. Lines 04-05 is a question-answer adjacency pair. Line 06 is an invitation. Therefore, the questioning in Line 04 is the FPP of a pre-invitation to check the availability of the invitee Cla. In Ex. 3, Lines 01- 02 is the pre-pre projecting that the base FPP is a request, which gets a go-ahead response in Line 03. Lines 04-05 is a question, by which the recognizability of the object to which Fred's request pertains is established. The work done in Lines 04-05 is called pre-mention to make sure that the recipient will recognize the reference or mention to be mentioned in the following talk. Once the recognizability is established, the projected action is initiated in Lines 07-09.

(2) Insert-expansion

Insert expansion refers to sequence expansion occurring between the base FPP and the base SPP. It can be divided into two types: post-firsts and pre-seconds (Schegloff, 2007) according to different interactional issues they address. Whereas post-firsts are repair sequences addressing problems in hearing or understanding of the preceding talk which are backward looking, pre-seconds are sequences clearing away obstacles for the base SPP in pending which are forward looking.

Ex. 4 (Cited from Schegloff, 2007: 102)
```
01  A:  Were you uh you were in therapy with a
02      private doctor?
03  B:  Yah.
04  A:  Have you ever tried a clinic?
05  B:  What?
06  A:  Have you ever tried a clinic?
07  B:  ((sigh)) No, I don't want to go to a clinic.
```
Ex. 5 (Cited from Sidnell, 2010: 104)
```
01  A:  May I have a bottle of Mich?
02  B:  Are you twenty-one?
03  A:  No
04  B:  No
```

In Ex. 4, Line 04 and 07 is the base adjacency pair – question-answer. Lines 05-06 is the insert-expansion, in which Line 05 is a next turn repair initiator and Line 06 is the repair solution. And it is what is called post-first (insert sequence) because this sequence solves a problem of hearing, which may interfere with the response to the question asked by A in Line 04. In Ex. 5, A makes a request in Line 01. B's next turn does not give any response; it asks a question, which is the FPP of the insert sequence. The question is in search of A's age as a precondition for responding to A's request, rather than dealing with a problem of hearing or understanding. B makes a rejection to A's request in Line 04 based on A's negative answer to B' question in Line 03. This insert expansion (Lines 02-03) is called a pre-second (insert sequence).

(3) Post-expansion

Post-expansion refers to sequence expansion occurring after the SPP of a base pair. According to Schegloff (2007), post-expansion is divided into minimal and non-minimal types. Minimal post-expansion offers an additional turn to the base SPP. The additional turn is used to close the sequence rather than initiating a new one, which is also termed sequence closing thirds (Schegloff, 2007), for instance, assessment, *Oh* (Heritage, 1984b) and *Okay* (Beach, 1993), etc. While non-minimal post-expansions are different in that the turn following that second pair part is itself a first pair part, and thereby projects at least one further turn – its responsive second pair part – and thereby its non-minimality (Schegloff, 2007: 149). There are various types of non-minimal post-expansions, for instance, other-initiated repair, topicalization, disagreement-implicated other-initiated repair, first pair part reworkings post-expansion and rejecting/challenging/disagreeing with the second pair part.

Ex. 6 (Cited from Schegloff, 2007: 121)
```
01  Ali:   You wan' me bring you anything?
02         (0.4)
03  Beb:   No: no: nothing.
04  Ali:   AW: kay.
```
Ex. 7 (Cited from Schegloff, 2007: 149)
```
01  Dee:   Well who'r you workin for.
02  Con:   · hhh Well I'm working through::
03         the Amfat Corporation.
04         (0.8)
05  Dee:   The who?
06  Con:   =Amfah Corpora[tion. (.)'ts a=
07  Dee:                 [Oh
08  Con:   =holding company.
09  Con:   Yeah
```

In Ex. 6, "Okay" in Line 04 is the acceptance of Beb's rejection to her offer and also serves to close this offer-rejection sequence. "Okay" is the minimal post-expansion, which is called sequence closing thirds. In Ex. 7, the question in Line 05 is an initiation of repair occasioned by the SPP of the question-answer sequence and gets its solution. The repair sequence (Lines 05, 06 & 08) is identifiable as a non-minimal post expansion, which ends with two minimal post-expansions.

3.3.2.3 Goings-in-front-of-an-action

There is one type of sequence, which is coming before the base sequence but does not project presence of the base sequence directly. It functions as a natural transition from the beginning of a conversation to the base FPP, which is named as goings-in-front-of-an-action. Like pre-sequences, goings-in-front-of-an-action is divided into two types: generic goings-in-front-of-an-action and type-specific goings-in-front-of-an-action (Yu & Liu, 2018).

(1) Generic goings-in-front-of-an-action

Generic goings-in-front-of-an-action are sequences subsequent to generic pre-sequence, which undertake to show attentiveness to the co-participants before the beginning of the base sequence and secure a good conversation atmosphere for prospective interactants moving to the next sequence. For instance, in Ex. 8 Lines 01-06 are summons-answer sequence and identification-confirmation sequence. The greeting-greeting sequence is what is called generic goings-in-front-of-an-action (Lines 07-11). Here the answer to the first "How are you" sequence is made (Line 08), and is followed by the reciprocal greeting initiated by R (Line 09). C's answer (Line 10) is followed by an assessment serving as sequence-closing thirds (Line 11). Greeting initiated by C is what is called the greeting exchange, showing attentiveness to the callee R, which also gets attentiveness from R by the reciprocal greeting. Both participants show fully preparation to the next sequence in the current conversation. The FPP of a base sequence or the FPP of a pre-sequence that could be initiated in Line 07 is withheld until the closure of the generic goings-in-front-of-an-action. Otherwise, the initiation

CHAPTER THREE RESEARCH METHODOLOGY

of the FPP may be taken to be too abrupt.

Ex. 8 (Cited from Schegloff, 1986: 115)

```
01       Ring
02   R:  Hello::,
03   C:  H'llo, Clara?
04   R:  Yeh,
05   C:  Hi. Bernie.
06   R:  Hi Bernie.
07   C:  How're you.
08   R:  I'm awright,
09   R:  How're you.
10   C:  Okay:?
11   R:  Good.
12   C:  Laura there?
```

(2) Type specific goings-in-front-of-an-action

Type specific goings-in-front-of-an-action having intrinsic relation with the base sequence projects the possible action-in-base-sequence to some extent. They could be goings-in-front-of-requests, goings-in-front-of-invitations, goings-in-front-of-tellings, etc. Type specific goings-in-front-of-an-action is designed to pave the way for the occurrence of the base sequence, which provides a cushion against abruptness and embarrassment of direct initiation of the base sequence. In Ex. 9, it seems that Lines 01-09 is a telling sequence, in which the pre-telling (Line 01) is followed by Don's troubles-reporting (Line 03, 05). "And " in Line 09 indicates that the sequence is continuing and is followed by Don's statement of his needs (Lines 11-13), which can be oriented to as projection of a request, soliciting Mar's help, although his request is not made explicitly. Mar's account for the rejection is evidence that she identifies Don's statement as a request. Thus, by goings-in-front-of-requests (Lines 01-15), the requester not only paves way for his request and makes it reasonable, but also even gets a pre-emptive answer without making it, although the answer is negative. It is obvious that Mar is unavailable, otherwise a pre-emptive offer could have provided. It also evidences that goings-in-front-of-requests has the function to solicit an offering, which is not always successful.

Ex. 9 (Cited from Schegloff, 2007: 64)

```
01   Don:    Guess what .hh
02   Mar:    What.
03   Don:    .hh My ca: r is sta:: lled.
04           (0.2)
05   Don:    ('n) I'm up here in the Glen?
06   Mar:    Oh:: .
07           {(0.4)}
08   Don:    {.hhh }
09   Don:    A: nd.hh
10           (0.2)
11   Don:    I don' know if it's po: ssible, but
12           {(.hhh)/(0.2)} see I haveta
13           open up the ba: nk. hh
14           (0.3)
15   Don:    a: t uh: (.)in Brentwood? hh=
16   Mar:    =Yeah: - en I know you want- (.) en
17           I whoa- (.)en I would, but- except
18           I've gotta leave in aybout
19           five min (h) utes. [ (hheh)
```

Bridging, another kind of type specific goings-in-front-of-an-action, seemingly has nothing to do with the base sequence but makes a trial on the closeness of the way to putting the request on board step by step. There is no exemplification of bridging, because this concept of going-in-front-of-an-action is put forward based on the Chinese data and it has not been found in the English data so far.

3.3.2.4 Turn design

Turn design refers to how a speaker constructs a turn-at-talk – what is selected or what goes into "building" a turn to do the action it is designed to do, in such a way as to be understood as doing that action (Drew, 2013a/b: 132). When s/he takes the turn, the speaker usually takes the following three aspects underlying turn design in to consideration: (1) what action will be performed through the turn; (2) how turns will be designed in order to implement the action and to display the connections between the current turn and the previous turn; and (3) how turns will be designed for a particular recipient at a particular sequential placement. Besides, both linguistic resources such as lexical, phonetic, prosodic, syntactic resources and other grammatical forms and non-linguistic resources including timing, laughter, aspiration, facial expression, gesture and other bodily movements are deployed in designing one's turns (Drew, 2013a/b).

3.3.3 Preference organization

In the vast majority of sequence types, there are not only alternative responses which a first pair part makes relevant and a recipient of a first pair part may employ; there are alternative types of response, and these embody different alignments toward the project undertaken in the first pair part (Schegloff, 2007: 58). The different types of responses to a FPP are not symmetrical alternatives (Schegloff & Sacks, 1973) and non-equivalent. The notion of preference is used to characterize these non-symmetrical alternatives, as explained by Atkinson and Heritage, the term "preference" here refers to the fact that, in conversation, choices between courses of action are routinely implemented in ways that reflect an institutionalized ranking of alternatives (Atkinson & Heritage, 1984: 53), rather than to speakers' personal or psychological desires. In preference organization, responses produced directly without delay are called preferred responses, while those made with delay, account or qualification are called dispreferred responses. Generally speaking, dispreferred responses have some basic features summarized as follows: (1) dispreferred responses are usually prefaced by delays, such as "well", "oh" etc. and sometimes inter-turn gap; (2) they are commonly accompanied by mitigation or attenuation, for example, "not" in "It's not too near." is designed to mitigate the distance; (3) they are also accompanied by palliatives like appreciation, apology and/or token agreement to attenuate "negative" valence of the dispreferred SPP, for example, It's so nice of you!; (4) accounts are often used to make explanations or justifications why a dispreferred SPP is made; and (5) pro forma agreement – agreement + disagreement is another way deployed, dispreferred SPP of this kind is usually begins with "yes, but ⋯" (Sidnell, 2010; Schegloff, 2007).

Preference can be classified into two types, one is related to the character of the course of the action and the other is related to grammatical structure or design of turns-at-talk (Schegloff, 1988 & 2007). The former has something to do with the successful realization of an action. For instance, the preferred SPP of an invitation is acceptance. But the latter more generally relies on the grammatical format, prosody, diction and other features of turn design (Schegloff, 2007). For example, the preferred SPP of a tag question "You are not busy now, are you?" is a negative answer.

Although we have introduced responsive actions namely SPPs in preference organization, it needs noting that there seems to be a preference for one kind of FPP over another kind among various FPPs. These two sorts of features – relationship to an underlying project or activity and the positioning and composition of the talk also appear to organize some alternative sets of FPPs (Schegloff, 2007: 81). For instance, a FPP of an offer sequence is preferred over a FPP of a request sequence. At the beginning of an interaction, a party to be recognized is preferred over to be self-identified. Compared with announcement-by-"self", there is a preference for noticing-by-others (Schegloff, 2007).

3.4 Research Procedures of the Present Study

In present study, one of the ubiquitous social actions – requesting is focused on. Unlike other methods, the present study neither takes categories or classes of actions named by terms as the starting point, nor analytically deconstructs them into the conceptual components which serve as the benchmarks for some particular action as an instance included in the corresponding class. Rather it begins with observation of some bit of talk, mainly taking three steps to make an analysis of requesting.

3.4.1 Observation and question formulation

I first examined the data at hand randomly and noticed that when people make a request, various syntactic formats, such as imperatives, declaratives, interrogatives, are used to carry out the action. Meanwhile, the action of requesting seldom occurs at the initial position of the sequence, instead, a pre-sequence frequently comes before the base sequence of requesting. The observed features of turn design and sequence organization engender my curiosity of uncovering the driving force that makes these features observable and the interactional consequence displayed by these features.

Then in order to find the answers to the above questions I began to collect more data in ordinary daily conversations and moved to the second step.

3.4.2 Data collection and transcription

In light of the discipline of CA that only naturally occurring conversations either from mundane life or institutional talk are to be examined as data, in the second procedure data from films, TV series, invented or fabricated conversations or experiments etc. are all excluded to keep actual reflection on real life. All the data collected in the present research are naturally occurring interactions from daily life including telephone conversations between family members, classmates, roommates, friends and colleagues in Mandarin Chinese. After data have been collected, recordings are transcribed in accordance with the system of transcription conventions developed by Gail Jefferson (1984) to represent details of talk-in-interaction as far as possible. The data of this study consists of 600 minutes audio-recorded conversations, in which 150 requesting sequences are identified. They are all transcribed in detail and checked and discussed in the data session by members of D. I. G. (Discourse and Interaction Group, a research group headed by Prof. Wu Yaxin and Prof. Yu Guodong primarily engaged in CA) to ensure the objectivity of all the transcripts.

3.4.3 Analysis

All the requests in the present study are an initiating action, which means it normatively requires a pair-typed responsive action: a granting or a rejection. The attention has been mainly paid to the design of the requesting turn and the organization of the requesting sequence. The syntactic formats and lexical choices of the requesting turn have been meticulous observed and investigated, and patterns have been identified and formally described. The expansion of the requesting sequence has also been analyzed and explicated.

CHAPTER THREE   RESEARCH METHODOLOGY

As afore-mentioned in Chapter One, being delicate is not a predetermined issue, instead, the delicacy of a certain topic is achieved interactionally by participants with certain conversational practices in the unfolding interaction. The conclusion has been drawn that the features displayed in both turn design and sequence organization of requesting are practices doing delicacy. The driving force that makes requesting a delicate matter is the maintenance of social solidarity.

3.5 Summary

To sum up, Conversation Analysis, an inductive and qualitative approach for studying language use in social interaction, has been introduced in this chapter. The content covers its origin and development, its leading principles, and its basic tools. The last part is the research procedures of the present study. The aim of a CA research is to discover and explicate practices by which speakers produce and hearers understand conduct in social interaction. Employing the analytical tools of CA method, the following chapters will concentrate on how delicacy is constructed and achieved by sequence organization and turn design of requesting.

CHAPTER FOUR   DELICACY IN SEQUENCE ORGANIZATION OF REQUESTING

As is well-known in pragmatic research, requesting is a face-threatening act, which threatens both the positive face of requesters when it is rejected and the negative face of requestees (Brown & Levinson, 1987). Therefore, pragmatic strategies are employed to reduce the face-threatening effect of requesting. Similarly, in conversation analysis, requesting is regarded as a dispreferred action due to the deferred occurrence of the requesting turn in the whole requesting sequence (Heritage, 1984a; Levinson, 1983; Robinson & Bolden, 2010; Schegloff, 1990; 2007; Taleghani-Nikazm, 2006). The pragmatic strategies of requesting are related to the turn design of requesting while the postponed requesting turn pertains to sequence organization. They all contribute to the achievement of delicacy of requesting. This chapter will focus on how delicacy of requesting is constructed in sequence organization.

4.1 Delicacy in Pre-expansion of Request Sequence

As afore-mentioned in Chapter Three, pre-expansions are sequences occurring before the base sequence and are measures undertaken by the speaker to check the possibility that a base sequence will be initiated (Schegloff, 2007: 29). It is divided into two types: generic pre-sequence

CHAPTER FOUR DELICACY IN SEQUENCE ORGANIZATION OF REQUESTING

and type-specific pre-sequence. In this section, how delicacy is constructed in two types of pre-expansion of request sequence – pre-requests and pre-pres will be discussed.

4.1.1 Delicacy in pre-requests

Pre-requests are composed of single or multiple adjacency pairs, used to check on the availability of a thing to be requested or the availability of the recipient where a service is being asked for (Sidnell, 2010: 103). As a practice often employed by requesters to initiate a request (Sacks, 1992a; Schegloff, 1980 & 2007; Levinson, 1983), pre-requests have two functions: to project the possible action implemented in the base FPP and to displace the action. It is the projectability of pre-requests that enables requestees to make a pre-emptive response, i.e. making an offer, to avoid the initiation of a request. Here are three examples.

Ex. 1 [DIG 16/ZJ/1: 0: 00]

(Jing and Shu who has a bicycle are friends. Wenying and Lingde are names of two canteens, of which Wenying is closer to the school gate.)

```
01    淑:    喂:? 咋了, 美女,
02           (0.9)
03    静:    喂:?
04    淑:    诶,
05           (1.0)
06    静:    你在不在学校了:
07    淑:    我在呢呀? 怎么啦?
08    静:    嗯: 上自习还是干嘛了.
09    淑:    我准备吃饭了这会儿hhh.
10           (1.2)
11    静:    准备吃饭了:=
```

12　淑：　＝嗯，你有事儿呢:?＝
13　静：　＝在文瀛?
14　淑：　我［还没过去呢，
15　静：　　　［（还是-）
16　静：　还是令德了．
17　淑：　还没［过去hhh．-
18　静：　　　［嗯，我- 我拿的- 我拿好多东西我回不去了，
19　　　　　我说让你过来，（．）我放你-（（笑））放你后面，
20　　　　　（（笑））
21　淑：　噢:［行，行行行，你在哪儿呢?

The first TCU *Hello* ("喂:?") in Line 01 and the un-transcribed telephone ring is the summons-answer sequence, which also is generic pre-sequence to secure the attention of the prospective participant. The TCU *what's up* ("咋了") asks about the reason for call and the TCU *the beauty* ("美女") indicates Shu (淑) has already identified the caller possibly from the phone number. Instead of introducing the reason for call, Jing (静) summons again to check whether Shu is on line (Line 03), which gets Shu's answer (Line 04). After one second gap, Jing asks a question about whether Shu is at school or not (Line 06). After a positive answer, Shu inquires about why Jing made such a question, which is what is called as post-pre[①] in CA (Line 07). Shu's question indicates that she has understood what Jing has asked about as preliminary to something else, but so far she cannot figure out what specific action is projected. Jing further asks about what Shu is doing by alternative question rather than answering her question (Line 08), neglecting the second sequential position for request-initiation. After saying yes to Jing's repair initiation (Line 11) on Shu's response in Line 09, Shu

---

① The post-pre is used to follow a pre-sequence whose projected action is unclear. It can be a response to the FPP of a pre-sequence and it also can follow a blocking response or a hedging response to the FPP of a pre-sequence to find out what it would have been (Schegloff, 2007).

CHAPTER FOUR   DELICACY IN SEQUENCE ORGANIZATION OF REQUESTING

makes an inquiry about Jing's reason for call again (Line 12). Without providing the reason for call once again, Jing asks shu where she will go for supper and receives a hedging answer (Lines 14 and 17 respectively). At this very moment, Jing talks about her reason for call (Lines 18-20).

The requester Jing checks the availability of Shu by three adjacency pairs (Lines 06-07, Lines 08-09 and Lines 13, 16-Lines 14, 17). The FPP of the three adjacency pairs involves three questions about the whereabouts of the requestee, what the requestee is doing or is going to do and the location where the requestee will go to. These questions are orderly arranged – the latter one is raised based on the answer of the former. If the answer to the first were a negative answer, the second question might be blocked. And if the second question were blocked, the third one and the request might be aborted. What is interesting in this example is that the requester (also the caller) does not deliver her reason for call (the initiation of the request) in the anchor position and she does not answer the requestee's question about her reason for call thrice. Not until the availability of Shu is ascertained, does the requester Jing make a request. She gives up the opportunity of making a request thrice and defers the delivery of her request, which helps to avoid a sequence with a rejected base SPP and which shows that initiating the request is proceeded with expressive caution by deferring the request until the appropriate sequential position, demonstrating altruism (Kendrick & Drew, 2016) in social interaction, which will be discussed in Chapter Six.

Ex. 2 [LS 19/BD/1: 0: 00]

(This is a conversation between Bai and Wen, two postgraduates under the same supervisor. Bai calls Wen to borrow a bicycle around 2 o'clock.)

```
01    白:    文文::
02           (0.8)
03    文:    嗯嗯>怎么啦<,
04    白:    你在睡觉吗?
```

05   (1.1)
06   文： 啊＞没有没有＜我- 我们正在开会呢，
07   (0.2)
08   白： 啊::＞在哪＜开会呢，
09   (0.4)
10   文： 嗯嗯，
11   白： 在哪开会呢，
12   (0.6)
13   文： 呃就在我- 这个呢:我们这个办公室就:＞就是这个＜
14   学院这个办公室［（孙老师他们-）
15   白：   ［问一下你有没有自行车:＄呵呵哼＄
16   (1.4)
17   文： （＞哎呀＜）那你过来吧张伟的在这呢，我一会给你
18   送下去.
19   白： 哦:我给他发了个微信他没理我，行行＞行行行＜

The above extract represents another function of pre-requests: to solicit an offer from the projected requestee and thereby to avoid production of a projected request. By calling Wen's name, Bai（白）mobilizes recipiency of Wen（文）（Line 01）, which is aligned by Wen's response *yeah*（"嗯嗯"）and *what's up*（"怎么啦"）functioning to ask the reason for call（Line 03）. Here, Line 04 is the first possible sequential position where the requester can deliver her goal of this call. Instead, passing over this opportunity to deliver her request, what is asked for by Wen, Bai asks whether Wen is sleeping（Line 04）, checking both whether Wen is disturbed possibly due to the time when this call is made and Wen's delayed response and whether he is in the dormitory as well. As a consequence, this has postponed her request-initiation. In the responding turn, the *no no*（"＞没有没有＜"）in a rushed way answers the question; the *we are having a meeting now*（"我- 我们正在开会呢"）provides more information than what is required（Line 06）.

CHAPTER FOUR   DELICACY IN SEQUENCE ORGANIZATION OF REQUESTING

Contingently Bai further asks about the meeting place, which is occasioned by Wen's response in the prior turn (Line 08). Possibly due to hearing problem, (Bai's WH-question is putatively heard as a confirmation seeking "you are in a meeting") Wen confirms with *yeah* ("嗯嗯") as a response to a confirmation seeking (Line 10), which triggers Bai's repetition of her question (Line 11). Having received the meeting place (Lines 13-14), Bai puts forward another question about whether Wen has a bicycle (Line 15), which hovers between a request and a pre-request (Clayman & Heritage, 2014: 69). Wen's pre-emptive offer as a response (Line 17-18), pre-empting Bai's need to do a request, is accepted by the prospective requester Bai (Line 19).

Note that, there are three pairs of pre-requests in this example (Lines 04-06, 08-14 & Line 15), which are presented in a progressive manner. The first two pairs aim to check the prospective requestee Wen's availability. Although the two questions in the first two pairs do not project a request is on the way, they pave the way for the third question [1] and prompt such a kind of understanding that they are used as preliminary to something else. This is evidenced by Wen's response displaying that he does not treat these two questions as two simple inquiries for information. The third one is used to check the availability of the requested object. At this moment, the floor is turned to Wen who has figured out what the action is preliminary to by these three questions, especially the third one, and pre-empts an offer. The sequential organization constructed illustrates the prospective requester's delicate design: the prospective requester passes over the first sequential position for request-initiation and simultaneously cautiously approaches the

---

[1] If the answer to the first question were yes, the second question might be about the bicycle possibly with sorry for having disturbed his sleeping. If the answer to the second question were a place out of the university, hinting that Wen is not at the university, the third question might be abandoned. And as it happens, the second question also displays the prospective requester Bai's highly monitoring of trajectory of the current sequence.

base action by launching pre-requests to check whether there are obstacles to the request's granting, resulting in not only deferring the initiation of the prospective request but also successfully soliciting an offer.

Ex. 3 [LS 16/ZXL/1:0:00]

(Shi and Jing are classmates living in the same domitory.)

```
01   诗：   诶:小晶姐,
02          (0.8)
03   晶：   嗯你去办公室了吗?
04   诗：   我在(.)宿舍呢,
05          (1.0)
06   晶：   噢↑:↓::噢:那就算了没事儿.
07   诗：   噢=
08   晶：   =(没有-)没有我找不见硬盘了我说是
09          .hh看看我硬盘在不在办公室了.没事儿=
10   诗：   =噢[:
11   晶：      [嗯我完了去看吧.
```

Compared with the above two examples, this example may demonstrate the delicate or cautious process of request-initiation more clearly. The availability is checked by pre-requests (Lines 03-04). Giving a non-conforming[①] response to Jing's question (namely, the FPP of the pre-requests), Shi (诗) provides the information about her whereabouts (Line 04). In doing so, Shi displays that she understood the prior turn (Line 03) not as a simple inquiry to

---

① Quesitons as FPPs make the relevant SPPs answers, and set constraints on ways of answering. For example, "who"-interrogatives make a person reference the relevant answer; "when"-interrogatives a time reference; "yes-no" interrogatives either yes or no and so on. There is a preference for type-conforming over non-conforming answers to "yes/no" interrogatives. In type-conforming responses, a speaker's stance toward the course of action initiated by a FPP is stated simply and straightforwardly (e.g., through a 'yes' or 'no,' which may be subsequently elaborated), while nonconforming responses specifically depart from the constraints embodied in the grammatical form of the FPP to produce an action not contemplated by it (Raymond, 2003:949).

CHAPTER FOUR   DELICACY IN SEQUENCE ORGANIZATION OF REQUESTING

seeking confirmation, but as preliminary to something yet-unspecified. The design of her question shows that Jing knows Shi's daily schedule, indexing a familiar relationship. The stretched *oh* ("噢↑:↓::噢:") registers a state-changing receipt of information (Schegloff, 2007: 119) followed by *Then forget it, that's ok* ("那就算了没事儿.") which displays that Jing (晶) aborts the articulation of a potentially projected action by metalanguage. What follows is *oh* ("噢") (a sequence-closing thrid) in service of possible closure for sequences (Schegloff, 2007) (Line 07) is latched by Jing's offer of her reason for call (Lines 08-09).

It seems that there is no request in the conversation. However, the riddle is revealed by Jing's reason for call, that is, the potential action to which the pre-sequence (Lines 03-04) is preliminary is a request. Therefore, the point here is that pre-requests display the requester's orientation to the avoidance of possibly negative response to a prospective base FPP – usually rejection to the request. The mobilization of pre-requests contributes to the understanding of the requester's doing delicacy in requesting sequences.

4.1.2   Delicacy in pre-pres

The pre-pre is preliminary to a preliminary or some preliminaries to the base FPP. They typically check whether a recipient will be able to recognize some person, place or thing to be talked about (Sidnell, 2010: 103), paving the way for the upcoming request, as in the following two instances.

Ex. 4 [MA 14/WN/2: 0: 00]

(Peng and Na who is a student majored in English are friends.)

01　娜：　啊？喂？
02　　　　(0.4)
03　鹏：　嗯:
04　娜：　嗯，［你说吧，

```
05    鹏：        ［诶，你干嘛了.
06    娜：        ［你现在-
07    鹏：        ［你们进入考试周了吗？
08              (0.3)
09    娜：       .hhh 就（.）差不多这两周吧. 嗯：反正：也：呃：
10              (才-) 有的考开啦.
11              (0.4)
12    鹏：       我是要提前跟你说一声＝现在还不用你帮忙,
13              .hhh 就是要过两天我要帮- 请你帮忙.
14              (0.3)
15    娜：       干嘛了,
16    鹏：       就是（.）.hhh 我们有一个专业英语的论文＝
17              ＝然后我写下了以后你稍微给我,＝
18              ＝.hhh 就是我（.）我觉得语法啦,
19              或者是词汇方面如果有问题让你给我（.）就是
20              <调：整一下>.
```

In this example, there is an elaborate pre-sequence of the base sequence, including pre-requests (Lines 05, 07-10) and the pre-pre (Lines 12-13). The pre-pre projecting the base FPP is a request *ask you a favor* ("请你帮忙") gets a go-ahead response (Line 15), a regular response to pre-pres. The space reserved by the pre-pre in Line 16 is used to introduce the object ("paper of English as a major"), to which Peng's request pertains. Only then does he convey the request that had been projected in the action projection of the pre-pre (Lines 12-13). In this example, the requester provides an opportunity for the requestee to reject the request projected by the pre-pre theoretically, which instead "setting up" a context in which information related to the projected request will be easily delivered. Consequently, rejection to a yet-to-be-delivered request is avoided. As a different kind of type-specific pre-sequence, the pre-pre is a practice

CHAPTER FOUR   DELICACY IN SEQUENCE ORGANIZATION OF REQUESTING

deployed by requesters to make a request. By the pre-pre, requesters not only leave room for requestees to respond but also protect oneself against being rejected, which demonstrates delicacy in requesting. In addition, pre-requests (Lines 05-10) are also used to check availability of the requestee. Sequentially speaking, both pre-requests and the pre-pre are used to help the requester delay the initiation of the request.

Ex. 5 [MA 14/YYF/5:0:00]

(Fei and Kang are former classmates. Fei is studying for a master's degree in another city, while Kang is still studying for his master's degree at the alma mater.)

```
01    飞：   喂,康康哥,是[我,
02    康：          [喂,
03    康：   嗯,[听出来啦,
04    飞：      [你能听出来不,听出来啦:？
05    康：   嗯[:
06    飞：     [嗯↑:↓:无事不登三宝殿呀,$呵呵 hhh $
07    康：   嗯,你说哇,$呵呵[$,
08    飞：              $呵呵[::hhh.$我想那啥=
09    康：                 [$呵$
10    飞：   =.hhh 我不是这两- 这(.)这会儿快转正啦？
11         然后我,我刚才给邢老师打了个电话,
12         想拿一下那个预备党员的考察表:
13         (0.6)
14    康：   嗯:=
15    飞：   =噢,我还说我下个星期回了,还打算让你给我订个房,
16         然后:后来老师说.hhh 他给寄哇.我一想,让 nia 寄
17         不太合适,
18         我就想要不让你给我°寄一下哇°
19    康：   嗯:行.
```

· 81 ·

The pre-pre (Line 06) is expressed in an idiomatic format to make clear that the base FPP is a request and gets a go-ahead response (Line 07). Fei (飞) introduces the background to which her request pertains (Line 08 and Lines 10-12), in which *what I want to do is* ("我想那啥") is used to defer the initiation of the request. In Line 10, a negative declarative is used to express a positive meaning, alerting to the recipient that a trouble may be forthcoming (Yu & Drew, 2017), and the same-turn self-repair from *this two- (days)* ("这两-（天）") to *recently* ("这会儿") blurs the time boundary reducing the imposition of the forthcoming request due to its urgency. After 0.6 second gap and a continuer ("嗯"), Fei goes on introducing the pre-condition which legitimizes her forthcoming request (Lines 15-17). It is the pre-pre that saves the space for introduction of background and pre-condition, which enables the sequence to proceed to the base FPP – initiation of a request (Line 18).

As an interactional device, the pre-pre can be deployed to make the request-initiation seamlessly achieved in such a trajectory: the pre-pre – the preliminary including pre-mentions or pre-conditions, or both – the request, demonstrating the delicacy in sequence organization of requesting. That is, the pre-pre projects that a request is in the offing by metalanguage, which provides an opportunity for the requestee to reject the projected request theoretically and which normally gets a go-ahead response leading to the preliminary. In the phase of preliminary, some person, place or background information relevant to the projected request will be delivered. If the requestee does not align with it, the prerequisite for granting the request would not exist. Therefore, the projected request would be aborted, in which case, a rejection to the request, a dispreferred response, would be avoided. It is the practices exploited to avert possible rejection of requests that demonstrate the delicacy of doing request.

CHAPTER FOUR DELICACY IN SEQUENCE ORGANIZATION OF REQUESTING

4.2 Delicacy in Goings-In-Front-Of-Requests

As has been introduced in Chapter Three, we have found another type of sequence which also comes before the base sequence but does not project the action type of the base sequence. When this type of sequence occurs before request sequence, it is named goings-in-front-of-requests. This sequence is not optional but interactional, that is to say, it plays certain interactional roles in the unfolding conversation. As a consequence of these roles, the delicacy of requesting is constructed.

4.2.1 Delicacy in generic goings-in-front-of-requests

Requesting, as a face-threatening action (Brown & Levinson 1978/1987) or a dispreferred action (Schegloff 2007), puts some imposition on the requestee. In telephone conversations, it is rare to initiate a request at the very beginning of the call. Pre-sequences are the common practice preceding the request sequence, but not the only practice. Sometimes sequences concerning the requestee's current situation occur before the request sequence buffing the abruptness of the initiation of requesting.

Ex. 6 [PZD 18/LSP/2:0:00]

(Ping and Dong are classmates.)

```
01    东:    喂,
02           (0.3)
03    平:    喂>兄弟<啊, 呃::[你把那个啥:论文交上了没呀,
04    东:                    [嗯,
05    东:    交啦:
06           (0.5)
07    平:    呃:(0.3)你有没有那个谁阿飞的电话号码.
```

08 东： 呃:有呢,
09   (0.3)
10 平： 那就给我发一下.[嗯,

Having assured of Dong's(东) attention(Line 01), Ping(平) straightforwardly prompts an inquiry about Dong's current state seemingly to find out how Dong is getting along. Ping's inquiry shows his concern for Dong. The kinship term bro("兄弟") used as address term, further suggests they have a close relationship or enables Ping to bond closer to Dong. After Dong's answering, the trajectory of the call diverts to a request sequence preceded by a gap.

(Lines 03 & 04) is a generic goings-in-front-of-requests, which is in the service of a transition to requesting and cushions abruptness and embarrassment in direct initiation of a request in the anchor position of a call. Following this sequence, still it is not the request turn proper, instead, a pre-request (Line 07) is used to check the availability of the requested item. The request is not made (Line 10) until the availability is assured (Line 08). Although forwarding a phone number costs little to the requestee, two types of sequences, namely, goings-in-front-of-requests and pre-request are still employed to postpone the request turn. These practices make the request hearably delicate.

Ex. 7 [PZD 18/LSP/1:0:00]

01 东： 喂,.tch
02 平： (.)你们今天干啥啊,
03 东： 宿舍呢,
04 平： 宿舍干啥忙- 闲着还是忙着啊,
05 东： 改论文么,
06   (0.4)
07 平： 你改的怎么样啊那是明天<u>一</u>定要交上来是哇,
08 东： ang,

CHAPTER FOUR   DELICACY IN SEQUENCE ORGANIZATION OF REQUESTING

```
09          (0.6)
10   平：   呃明天交的是电子版的还是那个::纸质版的也要交了呀,
11          (0.9)
12   东：   呀不清楚交不交纸的:
13          (0.9)
14   平：   ↑↓嗯::你-那个啥,(0.3)我(这会儿)在:在外面了?
15          (0.4)
16   东：   啥?=
17   平：   =那个:-手头紧张么给>我先<打上600块钱=
18          =我等一下晚上过来了我给你钱,
```

From Line 02 to 12 there are four pairs of inquiry-answer sequences. These inquiries from the caller are all about the current situation of the called, especially the first three inquiries. The fourth inquiry, which involves both the called and the caller, is occasioned by the third one. These inquiry-answer sequences do not project any specific action type of its following sequence. After a 0.9 second gap (Line 13), which is rather long interactionally and adumbrates the forthcoming action may be a dispreferred action, the caller Ping initiates his request "transfer me 600 yuan" in Line 17, before which there are delays ("那个啥", "那个") and accounts ("我（这会儿）在外面了", "手头紧张么"), and after which there is also a promise ("我等一下晚上过来了我给你钱"). Similar to the previous example, the abruptness of the request is moderated by the rather elaborate generic goings-in-front-of-requests (Lines 02-12 & "↑↓嗯::" at Line 14). The avoidance of direct initiation of requesting at the beginning of a phone call by a generic goings-in-front-of-request displays the process of requester's doing delicacy when a request is to be made.

Example 6 and 7 show that generic goings-in-front-of-requests by virtue of small talk plays a phatic role in communication, creating a friendly atmosphere and shortening the distance between a requester and a requestee, and cushions the initiation of a request, all of which exhibits that a requester is doing being delicate when initiating a request.

4.2.2　Delicacy in type-specific goings-in-front-of-requests

The so-called generic goings-in-front-of-requests is a post hoc concept since it does not project the action type of the forth-coming base sequence. But there do exist some types of sequences whose possible subsequent action is requesting. Troubles-telling sequence is one of them.

Ex. 8 [MA 11/LL/1:0:00]

(Ming and Bo are colleagues. They are washing machine salesmen.)

```
01  明：   嗨:博,(0.4)[你来了多久啦=
02  博：            [(    )
03  博：   =°哎呀°(0.7) 来了, 哎呀, 有个一年多了哇, (.)
04         咋啦,
05  明：   ((叹气)) 我这刚来感觉生意太::难做了,
06        (0.9)
07  博：   .tch 这（其实）不好做:? $没- 没有啥难$做的.
08        (.) 就是: 见- 见人说人话就行咧.
09        (1.4)
10  明：   感觉好难卖出去呀, 这提成根本就拿不了多少. (0.3)
11        靠这靠这死工资根本不行.
12  博：   哦提成啊,
13        .hhh 其实你看啊咱卖洗衣机=提成你就不要卖那种
14        双缸的=它提成太少=你就- 推高端机, 它就(0.8)
15        挣钱多, 提成高么. 下回来了顾客,
16        你就往那个滚筒那儿引就行啦.
17        (3.3)
18  明：   要不下次你:: 我卖的时候你指导指导我在我身边,
```

CHAPTER FOUR　DELICACY IN SEQUENCE ORGANIZATION OF REQUESTING

19　　　　(1.1)
20　明：　(　) 我请你吃饭?
21　博：　哦,没事,下回你就- >你跟的你跟的<
22　　　　你这两天看的就行了.

Similar to Ex. 6, the conversation opens up with the generic goings-in-front-of-requests (Lines 01-04) ended with *what's up* ("咋啦") which inquires about the reason for Ming's (明) question in Line 01 and which is an evidence (to Ming and to us as well) that Bo (博) has recognized that Ming's question is not just a simple question about his working experience, but a spring board to further social actions. Instead of answering Bo's question, Lines 05-16 is a troubles-telling sequence, one type of goings-in-front-of-requests, in which, Ming is reporting his trouble from general to specific (Lines 05 & 10-11), successfully soliciting Bo's advice twice (Lines 08, 13-16). Ming does not take Bo's first advice, and after 1.4 seconds gap, he specifies his trouble by extreme case formulation (Pomerantz, 1986) ("根本不行") to index the seriousness of his trouble, which gets Bo's another detailed advice (Lines 13-16). Ming does not take Bo's advice again. And after 3.3 seconds gap, he delivers a request (Line 18).

In this example, the requester makes a request after the generic goings-in-front-of-requests and the troubles-telling sequence, namely the goings-in-front-of-requests, which is different from afore-mentioned pre-requests. In the troubles-telling sequence (Jefferson, 1988), the FPP is a statement of one's trouble; the possible SPP may be advice or offering. In this example, the two pieces of advice as response to the troubles-telling seemingly do not handle the requester's trouble. The requester initiates a request after the second advice (Line 18). If the requestee had offered help, the request would not have been made. As the initiative action, requesting is treated as a dispreferred action, while offering a preferred action (Schegloff, 2007). Therefore, the troubles-telling sequence as the goings-in-front-of-requests not only delays the initiation of requests sequentially but also has a potential function to solicit help from the co-participant, so that requesting might be averted.

Ex. 9 [MA 14/CXK/4:0:00]

(Kai and Pai are friends.)

01　凯：　喂，小排，
02　　　　(0.3)
03　排：　诶，那个你拿上那个快递啦？=
04　凯：　=嗯，拿上啦，你回宿舍啦？
05　　　　(0.6)
06　排：　没呢没呢，我和我弟在外面，我俩想那个
07　　　　看个电影了. 但 [是我的手机在这团不上，你在宿舍不.
08　凯：　　　　　　　　[嗯::
09　凯：　嗯（呵呵）在呢.
10　　　　(0.6)
11　排：　你能不能帮我团一下呀=就在美团，

After the summons-answer sequence and identification and recognition sequence (Lines 01-03), Pai (排) initiates a generic goings-in-front-of-requests sequence, showing attentiveness to Kai (凯) (Lines 03-04). And Kai gives an answer to it and does the reciprocal by *Did you go back to your dorm* ("你回宿舍啦？"). Pai not only gives a reply but also offers more information than What Kai asked, namely her trouble to book film tickets, plus a question whether Kai is at dormitory or not (Lines 06-07). It is the first sequential position and the initial opportunity for Pai to initiate her request in Line 07, but she chooses to tell her trouble, which functions as the FPP of the goings-in-front-of-requests and provides an opportunity to Kai to make offering, and produces the FPP of a pre-sequence to check Pai's availability, which is the precondition to make a request and also is the second position to issue her request. But Kai only answers about her

CHAPTER FOUR DELICACY IN SEQUENCE ORGANIZATION OF REQUESTING

whereabouts without offering help or advice. If Kai's answer at Line 09 were negative, Pai's request (Line 11) would possibly not be made. Although troubles-telling in this example does not solicit an offer, it defers requesting and also functions as an account legitimizing the request. Here the combined use of both generic and type-specific goings-in-front-of-requests again demonstrates the delicate nature of doing requesting.

Different from troubles-telling sequence, which is a natural transition from troubles-telling to requesting, especially when the trouble has not been solved yet in the troubles-telling sequence, another type of type-specific goings-in-front-of-requests is doing favorable social actions to the requestee, such as showing gratitude, inviting, offering, etc., which paves the way to the initiation of requesting. For convenience of illustration, this type is named bridging.

Ex. 10 [MA 14/DY/1:0:00]

01	丽：	学姐？打扰一下，你现在方不方便了.
02	艳：	嗯,你进来吧,什么事呀,
03	丽：	嗯:那个我就是想问一下你那个关于考研的事情么.
04		那个你们当时考研的时候看了哪些书呀.
05	艳：	就我给你(.)当时发邮箱里面那些书,看了就行啦.
06	丽：	嗯:那几本就行?=
07	艳：	=嗯,够- 够啦,那几本足够啦,
08		现在时间紧迫,不要看那些没有- 不重要的书,拣重
09		点的看.
10	丽：	哦::行,
11		哎呀,那这段儿时间麻烦你啦:谢谢你啊.
12	艳：	嗯:没事没事 =
13	丽：	=那:我想:咱们:请你吃个饭,
14	艳：	>别别别别<小事一桩,何必客气,不吃饭((笑))=
15	丽：	=哎呀,那多不好意思 [了呀,

16 艳: [嗯::没事.
17 丽: 那个:呃::我其实是还有另外一件事情,
18   就是:我想看一下你的那个笔记.

There are two episodes of sequences before requesting in this extract. Sequence One is Lines 01-10, in which Li（丽）is inquiring about how to prepare for the entrance examination for postgraduates and Yan（艳）answers it. Sequence Two is Lines 11-16, in which Li is extending thanks to Yan orally and making an invitation to express her gratitude again, but Yan refuses the invitation. It seems that Sequence One and Sequence Two are asking for guidance and expressing gratitude respectively, but they are actually bridges to requesting (Lines 03-16). It is irreproachable that Li asks Yan for advice because Yan took the exam one year earlier than Li. But note that Yan's response in Line 05, which displays that Li had consulted Yan and got the answer. So it is superfluous that Li makes such an inquiry again. Yan makes a re-confirmation to Li's question and provides accounts making her answer reasonable (Lines 07-09). Under such circumstances, Li has no choice but to accept Yan's answer, which moves to Sequence Two – extending her gratitude to Yan. In the face of rejection to her invitation (Lines 14, 16), Li expresses her purpose – to borrow Yan's notebook. Li's request is positioned subsequent to gratitude-showing and invitation sequences, namely bridging, which is one of the typical practices used by Chinese conversationalists before making a request.

Ex. 11 [MA 15/LHL/2:0:00]

01 军: 你们还不睡觉?
02 红: .hh(0.4)嗯::睡吧:我就是给你打个电话问一下
03   你怎么样了,安顿好了没.
04   (0.8)
05 军: 啊,其实已经:弄好了.
06   (1.4)

CHAPTER FOUR   DELICACY IN SEQUENCE ORGANIZATION OF REQUESTING

```
07    红：    哎呀：hhh.（0.3）哎呀完了给你买个早点儿的车吧：
08            你这要是回北京的话,.hhh 这么晚可咋弄啊＝
09    军：    ＝((醒鼻子))
10            (2.1)
11    军：    °哎呀：° 到时候再说吧，现：现买吧.
12    红：    嗯：＝
13    军：    ＝现在我还［真不知道-
14    红：              ［↑完了.反正：那个什么你最好提前把你
15            的(.)行程告我＝就差不多你要- 呃：差不多知道什么
16            时候要走的时候,.hhh 然后把你的＞行程告诉我＜
17            然后我提前给你买吧. ＞哎呀妈呀＜
18    军：    嗯：
19    红：    ＞不行＝你得给我打钱＝我我我没钱给你买票啦,
20            我已经没钱啦＜我真：的已经没钱啦.
21            (1.1)
22    军：    行, 回头我给你打吧因为现在：：我- 我那卡里面也
23            ＞没了＜
```

In this conversation Hong (红) and Jun (军) are in a romantic relationship. Line 01 is the initiation of a pre-closing, and the first TCU of Line 02 is a reciprocal pre-closing("嗯：：睡吧：") and the second TCU of Lines 02-03 is a formulation summarizing what they have been talking to each other (Heritage & Watson, 1979). Line 05 is a confirmation of the prior formulation. At this point, it is a proper place to end the conversation. But after a long gap (Line 06) the caller Hong initiates a new sequence instead of closing the conversation. This new sequence is an offering sequence (Lines 07-17). The first offer is made in Line 07 accompanied by an account (Line 08). This offer is rejected (Line 11) with an interrupted account (Line 13), which is met with Hong's interruption prompting a pursuit of her offer (Lines 14-17). Compared with the first offer, this offer is in a rather elaborate version, including the time when to tell her the return time and his itinerary (Lines 15-16). Then note that, directly after the second offer is made (Line 17), an interjection ("哎呀妈呀") in a compressed way is produced signaling what follows is a sudden awareness and is occasioned by the previous talk. As it happens, getting Jun's continuer (Line 18), the talk successfully proceeds to requesting, which unmasks her offer.

Similar to Ex. 10, Hong's request is made after the bridging (Lines 07-17), in which Hong is making an offer. It apparently displays that the offer sequence – the bridging functions more to cushion the upcoming request by showing attentiveness and interest to the co-participant. The subtlety of bridging is that it plays a helpful role in assisting the requester in initiating a request in a friendly atmosphere. Each step of bridging paves the way for initiating a request.

4.3　Summary

The present chapter offers a detailed description of how requesters construct delicacy of requesting sequentially. Delicacy is not a given feature of requesting sequence but a constructed interactional reality in requesting sequence. The occurrences of pre-sequences and goings-in-front-of-requests objectively defer the initiation of requesting sequentially. The availability of the requested person or objects checked by the pre-sequences and the pre-conditions and background information related to the request provided by the pre-pres all reduce the possibility of a forth-coming request being rejected. The concerns to the requestee shown by the generic goings-in-front-of-requests and the favorable actions delivered by the requester to the requestee in the type-specific goings-in-front-of-request all lubricate the interpersonal relationship between the interlocuters and facilitate the issuance of the request. All the work done by the requester before making a request demonstrates that

CHAPTER FOUR DELICACY IN SEQUENCE ORGANIZATION OF REQUESTING

requesting is not a simple and easy job but a delicate and intricate one.

Besides sequence organization, turn design is the other locus where delicacy is constructed. The delicacy in the turn design of requesting is the next topic we now turn to.

CHAPTER FIVE   DELICACY IN TURN DESIGN OF REQUESTING

This chapter will continue exploring the establishment of delicacy of requesting by focusing on the turn design of requesting. Specifically, how requests are initiated and how initiations of requests are treated as delicate issues by focusing on the turn design. This chapter will offer a description of how different interactional devices are deployed in the turn design of requesting to construct delicacy in requesting and to allow the requestee to accurately ascribe or identify that requesting is being performed at the moment in a somewhat delicate way.

5.1   Deferring the Requests

Requesting is not only postponed sequentially as afore-mentioned in Chapter Four, but also deferred in terms of its turn design. Two ways of delay are observed: requesting can be delayed by turn initial delay (Silverman & Peräkylä, 1990; Weijts, Houtkoop & Mullen, 1993) and other actions as preface for the upcoming request. These practices can be used separately or in combination.

5.1.1   Turn initial delays

Rather than being delivered at the very beginning of the turn, requests

CHAPTER FIVE DELICACY IN TURN DESIGN OF REQUESTING

are frequently prefaced by some particles ("嗯", "呃"), or demonstratives ("那个", "那个啥"), which are sometimes elongated. These practices postpone the occurrence of the request proper interactionally and occur at the initial position of the turn, so they are termed as turn-initial delays. Consider the following two examples.

Ex. 1 [MA 14/WM/8: 0: 00]
01 梦： 喂:?
02   (1.1)
03 菲： 喂:?
04 梦： 嗯，干嘛呢,
05 菲： 睡觉吗?
06   (0.9)
07 梦： 躺着呢，干嘛呢,
08   (0.5)
09 菲： 嗯::你下午要是有空的话帮我去取一下快递吧.

Turn initial delay, a feature of the dispreferred organization (Pomerantz, 1984; Pomerantz & Heritage, 2013), is one of the common practices used by interactants to deal with delicate issues. In this example, the elongated *en* ("嗯:"), without semantic meaning, starts the request turn while simultaneously delaying the delivery of the request. It also displays the requester's hesitancy to initiate her request. Hesitating in this way is also observed in the following example.

Ex. 2 [LS 17/LAX/5: 0: 00]
16 东： 喂,
17 雄： 喂老彭::
18 东： 嗯.
19   (1.0)
20 雄： 起来啦:
21   (0.4)

22　东： 没呢 hh.
23　　　(1.2)
24　雄： 呃:::那- 那个实验室的钥匙我:上来取一下哦等会儿.
25　　　(0.3)
26　东： ˚呃嗯 hhh.

Similar to Ex. 1, the elongated *e* ("呃:::") in Line 24 enables the requester Xiong (雄) not only to hold the floor but also to defer the delivery of the request proper. Besides, the elongation of *e* ("呃:::") functions as a signal of the requester's hesitancy to initiate his request.

Besides the particles ("嗯", "呃"), the delivery of requesting could also be deferred by producing perturbations. A perturbation can be a pause, a hesitation (such as "嗯" "呃", "那个", "那个啥", "就是", etc.) or a self-repair, manifesting disfluency of a turn at talk.

Ex. 3 [LS 17/HB/1:0:00]
01　冰： 喂,
02　茹： 喂:? 韩咩咩是我:hhh.
03　冰： 诶:我知道呀?
04　茹： .hhh 呃那个啥, 你:你给我发一个就是:那个杨松老师的
05　　　 电话呗.(.).hhh [我们打扫卫生呢,
06　冰：　　　　　　　　[杨松?
07　茹： 嗯好像是[他在负责呢, 噢:找不到他, [给他打个电
08　　　 话现在.

In this example, the turn initial particle ("呃") is used together with another type of filler *nagesha* ("那个啥") in Line 04 to preface the upcoming request. The demonstrative word *that* ("那个") in Line 04 loses its demonstrative function because it does not have a specific reference. The kind of perturbations functions to delay the completion of the initiation of Ru's request.

Ex. 4 [PZD 17/LAX/1:0:15]
15　雄： 我我早::你把钥匙-(.)你把钥匙给我吧我早早过去=

CHAPTER FIVE DELICACY IN TURN DESIGN OF REQUESTING

16   =因为:那个啥(.) 我们一块儿人家要做那个啥
17   (.) 要做容量瓶了嘛=我 [拿回来的.

In Line 15, before initiating a request, the requester is doing searching by a set of perturbations (including hesitation ("我我早::"), self-repair ("我我早::你把匙-(.)你把钥匙给我吧我早早过去") and a micro pause (.)) at the beginning of the turn. The perturbations show that the request is delivered in a hesitating manner, thereby displaying the requester's orientation toward appropriateness or propriety in initiating the request. Thus, perturbations are perhaps evidence that the requester is with expressive caution (Silverman, 2001) dealing with the requesting as delicate.

5.1.2 Other actions-prefaced requests

The delivery of requesting may also be preceded with other actions, as is shown in the following two cases.

Ex. 5 [HB 16/ZY/1:0:00]
01   冰: .hhh 喂,
02   (0.4)
03   瑜: 韩冰呀,
04   冰: 诶.
05   瑜: 你在宿舍吗?
06   冰: 在了呀,
07   (0.5)
08   瑜: 你帮我个忙,((笑))=
09   冰: =你说,
10   瑜: 每天就这点儿破事儿,我刚回来又有事儿,
11   你帮我从那个:(0.6) 就是.hhh 放键盘的那个
12   抽屉里面找,找一- 找一下那个(.) 我的一寸照片儿,
13   (1.1)

14　冰：　　＜放键盘的这个＞噢：=

Lines 10-12 is the request turn. Note that Yu（瑜）could have initiated a request in Line 10, instead, she passes it. This is the place where delicacy is attended to by Yu. Note further that the initiation of the request is retarded by adding the complaint（Line 10）. By the extreme case formulations（Pomerantz, 1986）("每天","刚…又…"), the complaint is designed to make her complaint complainable. By producing the complaint first, the requester leaves it up to the requestee to consider what will be or might be projected next and somehow justifies the upcoming request with a claim of uncontrollable circumstances.

Ex. 6 [MA 14/LH/3:0:00]

01　柳：　　诶:（0.6）在哪了.
02　　　　（1.1）
03　昊：　　宿舍.
04　柳：　　噢::你一会吃饭不=帮我取个快递吧=我在医院呢.

In Line 04, *oh*（"噢::"）serves as a sequence-closing third（Schegloff, 2007）. On the closure of the prior sequence, a new FPP – a request composed of multi-unit is initiated. What marks it as delicate is the addition of the pro-forma pre-request（"你一会吃饭不"）which will be the focus here and the account（"我在医院呢"）which will be the focus of the next section. Both the projection of the pre-request to the request and the placement of the pre-request and the request allow them to be constructed in such a package of "pre-request + request". This kind of format constitutes another request-delaying practice. Note that the pro-forma pre-request initiates a new sequence, which is subsequent to the completion of the prior sequence, but it is simultaneously related to the prior one in activity and in relevance. It is the pro-forma pre-request that functions to delay the request proper. It also serves as a link between the prior sequence and the following request proper.

CHAPTER FIVE DELICACY IN TURN DESIGN OF REQUESTING

As it demonstrates, the above practices used in deferring requests show that how the request proper is proceeded cautiously and delicacy is locally marked and managed.

5.2 Accounts

The afore-mentioned practices accomplish construction of delicacy in requesting by deferring delivery of the request proper. It is accounts that are another practice to achieve constructing delicacy in turn design of requesting. An account means a statement made by a social actor to explain unanticipated or untoward behavior – whether that behavior is his own or others', and whether the proximate cause for the statement arises from the actor himself or from someone else. Accounts are classified into two types: justifications and excuses. The former are accounts in which one accepts responsibility for the act in question, but denies the pejorative quality associated with it, and the latter are socially approved vocabularies for mitigating or relieving responsibility when conduct is questioned (Scott & Lyman, 1968: 46-47). Accounts can be designed in different sequential positions in requesting. Here, the attention is paid to accounts placed in the turn of requesting as in the following cases.

Ex. 7 [PZD 17/LAX/1: 0: 06]

(Dong, the keeper of the key to the laboratory, and Xiong have been doing experiments in the same laboratory. Xiong calls Dong to borrow the key the night before the experiment scheduled for the following day. The following conversation begins after identification and recognition has been achieved.)

```
09    雄：  诶那个:::实验室钥匙你明天去不去啊.
10    东：  嗯:我明天去呢.
11          (0.8)
12    雄：  早上几点啊.
```

```
13        (0.8)
14  东：  早上::: (0.6)九点［多吧.
15  ?：              ［(    )
16  雄：  我我早::你把匙-(.)你把钥匙给我吧我早早过去=
17        =因为:那个啥(.)我们一块儿人家要做那个啥(.)
18        要做容量瓶了嘛=我［拿回来的.
19  ?：                  ［(    )
20        (0.6)
21  东：  嗯:你做实验呢明天,
```

With certainty about the availability of Dong(东), Xiong(雄) initiates the request in the imperative format (Line 16). The request in this example is connected by two accounts, in which the former one is for the request, while the latter is used to account for both the former one and the request proper. The first account I'll go to the lab *early in the morning* ("我早早过去")(Line 16) belongs to the type of excuses, explaining why he needs the key. It explicitly presents the fact by invoking one's inability due to the fact shared between the two participants (that he is not the person keeping the key and common sense that the one who keeps the key is obligated to provide the key to others when they need it). Therefore, although it seems that it contradicts to the no fault quality (Heritage, 1984a), a known feature of many accounts in interaction, it justifies his request in terms of alleviation of the requester's responsibility and affirmation of his entitlement to initiate this request to some degree. However, this is not the end of the story. This account continues by another one with the causal connective *because* ("因为")(Line 17). Different from the first one, agency in the second account which also serves as an excuse is attributed to *we* ("我们") and *they* ("人家")(which refers to other members in a group rather than Xiong himself.) At the same time, the details are also presented, including the type of the equipment associated with the experiment to be done the next day and the

CHAPTER FIVE DELICACY IN TURN DESIGN OF REQUESTING

person who brought the equipment back. All information is introduced by the causal connective underlining the casual relation between the two parts connected by *because* (Lines 17-18). In this way, Xiong explains that both the initiated request and the first account are the result of the second one, being the result of the decision made by a group (we) rather than Xiong himself. And simultaneously, he also explicitly identifies the beneficiary, the whole members who will participate in the experiment, instead of Xiong himself. Thus, the second account functions to distance himself from associated responsibility for producing the request and also constructs himself as a kind and helpful person.

Although the account is lengthy, what can be noticed here is that the way in which the requester holds the floor (using "because"), establishes himself as a representative for the whole members and justifies the initiated request retrospectively. This example provides a case of accounting that the requester is highly attentive to managing untowardness of the request and making the request reasonable. However, in some examples an account in the service of the similar function is positioned before the request proper. The example below is a case in point.

Ex. 8 [LS 18/ZHF/1:0:00]

(This conversation is between Fang and Dong, one of the key keepers. Upon finding the laboratory inaccessible, Fang asks Dong if he could open the door.)

15　东：　喂，
16　芳：　.hhh 呃那个(.)实验室的钥匙是不是你拿着呢，
17　东：　呃：hhh.
18　芳：　呃那个啥.hhh 今天吴老师过来看要我们做实验，
19　　　　那个你能过来把门开一下吗，

After turn initial delay and hearable inbreath, the account (Line 18), like the second account in Ex. 7, foregrounds the management of her

· 101 ·

untoward or unanticipated requesting. By explicitly presenting the fact (that they will carry out experiments under the supervision of Ms. Wu.), Fang (芳) attributes to the third party's agency by which both the supervisor's responsibility for guiding students' learning and all members as the beneficiary (Clayman & Heritage, 2014) of her upcoming request are invoked. The account not only postpones the delivery of the request to a certain degree but also furnishes the forthcoming request with reasonable grounds; accordingly, it prospectively justifies the request and also distances herself from the responsibility for initiating her request.

Account-giving displays the requester's awareness of the unexpected or dispreferred nature of requesting. As demonstrated in Ex. 7 and Ex. 8, by embedding accounts into the request turn either prior to or subsequent to the request proper, the requester manages the untowardness of requesting, thereby showing how delicacy is made visible in designing the request turn. Additionally, accounts also implicitly index a beneficiary-benefactor relationship in requesting.

5.3　Appreciation

A third practice that requesters use to construct delicacy when initiating a request is acknowledging a distribution of benefits or costs (Clayman & Heritage, 2014) associated with requesting and compensating for requestees' costs to granting of the request. This is illustrated in the following example, which is a truncated version of Ex. 8 in Chapter Four. Recall that Bo's two pieces of advice are provided as response to Ming's troubles-telling. Not having accepted Bo's advice, Ming initiates a request in Line 16.

Ex. 9 [MA 11/LL/1: 0: 44]

16　明：　要不下次你::我卖的时候你指导指导我在我身边,
17　　　　(1.1)

CHAPTER FIVE   DELICACY IN TURN DESIGN OF REQUESTING

```
18   明：  （  ）我请你吃饭？
19   博：  哦，没事，下回你就- >你跟的你跟的<
20        你这两天看的就行了.
```

Notice that beginning with *or* ("要不"), the request is launched in a tentative way. At this point, Ming's turn reaches possible completion in terms of syntactic, intonational and pragmatic completion (Clayman, 2013; Ford & Thompson, 1996), leading to a possible TRP. But insofar as the contiguity (Sacks, 1987) between Ming's request and Bo's granting/rejection is broken up by the 1.1-second gap (Line 17), which may be understood as projection of an incipient rejection and provides Ming an opportunity to do remedial work (Goffman, 1971). Orienting to this gap, Ming continues his request by providing an invitation as appreciation, which could counterbalance Bo's costs to some extent. By such an appreciative invitation, the requester not only identifies himself and Bo as the beneficiary and benefactor of the requesting respectively, but also reciprocates Bo's costs. Obviously, this maneuver successfully gets granting as response, thereby warding off face-threats and avoiding a dispreferred response, which will allow the response to be delivered as a preferred response rather than a dispreferred one. In so doing, the requester is initiating requesting and simultaneously doing something "extra" – doing delicacy.

Besides appreciation in the request turn, there are other methods for acknowledging a distribution of benefits and/or costs in requesting, which will be discussed in Section 5.4.

5.4   Index of a Distribution of Benefits and/or Costs Associated with Requesting

When delivering requesting, requesters usually index a distribution of benefits and/or costs associated with requesting by minimal portrayal of requesting, minimization of costs of requesting to requestees or maximization of benefits of requesting to requesters. These three ways share a commonality that warding off face-threats and influencing the likelihood of granting.

5.4.1 Minimal portrayal of requesting

Requesters have a tendency to portray their requesting as minimal costs to requestees. Two different ways are observed – avoidance and masqueraded requesting.

5.4.1.1 Avoidance

The notion of avoidance[①] is drawn from the study of Weijts, Houtkoop and Mullen (1993). Here it refers to ways such as doing request without explicitly saying it by which the link between requesters and the action of requesting is obscured or loosened.

Ex. 10 [MA 14/DY/8:0:00]

01	白:	王梦::?
02	梦:	嗯:? 干嘛?
03		(0.5)
04	白:	你饿不饿?
05		(0.8)
06	梦:	还好,我刚才吃了点.
07	白:	刚才吃的:?
08	梦:	嗯,我刚才出去买了点.
09	白:	都六点啦:((笑)) .hhh hhh.
10		(0.5)
11	白:	$刚才是刚才,该吃晚饭啦:$

---

① Avoidance is a strategy used when delicate issues relating to sexuality are talked about in medical consultations. It includes ways of using vague terms, omitting delicate terms or using pronous (Weijts, Houtkoop & Mullen, 1993:304) by which delicate terms relating to sexuality is avoided.

CHAPTER FIVE DELICACY IN TURN DESIGN OF REQUESTING

12　梦： 嗯：一会儿的吧. 我刚才吃了点现在（.）不太饿.
13　白： 那你一会儿饿不饿？
14　梦： 我一会儿还要出去呢＝
15　白： ＝＞你<u>去哪儿</u>？＜
16　　　 （0.4）
17　梦： 食堂：
18　白： 哎呀，太棒啦，也就是说：是哇？（（笑））
19　　　 （0.6）
20　梦： 噢：你是：：？
21　　　 （0.4）
22　白： 对，我是.
23　　　 （0.5）
24　梦： 嗯，我- 我帮你稍点是哇＝
25　白： ＝＞对对对对对对对对＜

Based on the management of the lengthy pre-requests so as to attempt to fish for an offer (Lines 04-17), Bai (白) makes the request without explicitly saying it (Line 18). Her positive assessment, registering information receipt, can be understood as projection of what comes to be treated by Bai as an action having something to do with Meng's (梦) answer. Bai's omitted utterance *That is to say* ("也就是说：") plus a somewhat likely tag-type item *Doesn't it* ("是哇？") in rising tone makes it hearably seeking confirmation that you know what I really mean and invites Meng to supplement the omitted part. In this way, Bai delays progression of her aimed action and simultaneously places Meng in the position of figuring out (Line 20) and pointing out what she is doing (Line 24). Hence, requesting is somehow transformed into offering.

The way of making a request only sensed, not expressed in words, could be considered an effective practice to deal with delicate issues. That is, instead of making a request explicitly, requesters leave room for requestees to do this job. Therefore, requesting is an interactional achievement by both the requester and the requestee, with the effect of saving face of both sides. It is the way that delivering a request by requestee's mouth that dynamically adumbrates the process of constructing delicacy in requesting, which is in line with both Lerner's (2013) and Yu and Wu's (2015) findings respectively – the delicate way to treat delicate matters: delaying the initiation of the matter and furnishing the opportunity for the recipient to mention the delicate.

Ex. 11 [PZD 18/HZL/1:0:00]

```
01       (0.3)
02  东： 喂,
03       (0.7)
04  黄： 嗯.
05  东： 唉小黄你在哪儿呢 h.
06       (0.6)
07  黄： 我在宿舍.
08       (0.4)
09  东： 诶- 我的那个充电器：是不是落宿舍啦 hh.
10       (2.6)
11  黄： <充电器>
12  东： ang 手机充[电器么.
```

This example involves an implicitly unsaid request. The question is the vehicle for requesting (Line 09). From the perspective of epistemics (Heritage, 2012), the epistemic asymmetry between Dong (东) and Huang (黄) is based on the precondition that Huang is at the dormitory (Line 07). This cue provides evidence that Dong's question, seemingly information-seeking, will result in another action – Huang has to do an action to find out whether Dong's charger is at the dormitory. Or put simply, it is not only requesting for information, but also asking Huang to find out the information. In this way, requesting is produced avoiding explicitly saying it.

CHAPTER FIVE   DELICACY IN TURN DESIGN OF REQUESTING

These two examples illustrate how minimal portrayal of requesting is achieved, getting requesting successfully done without explicitly "doing" it.

5.4.1.2 Masqueraded requesting

Masqueraded requesting is a more interesting case in which the nature of requesting is disguised in other actions as to reduce costs to requestees. Masqueraded requesting can be only achieved through exploiting the distribution of benefits and/or costs associated with requesting.

Ex. 12 [MA 15/YJW/2: 0: 40]

This exchange occurs between two classmates who are talking about what Li (丽) did at home during the three-day holiday. The "offer" at Line 25 is occasioned by the information that Li bought a new laptop delivered in the previous talk.

```
20    光：    你真买的°是-°那个十块钱的？
21    丽：    (          ) 没有，[买了-
22    光：                      [我（怀疑）你买了个电脑呢，
23            (0.8)
24    丽：    就是买了个电脑么.
25    光：    噢买个电脑(.)不- >设置好不好< 要不然我帮你玩
26            儿玩儿啊.
27            (1.4)
28    丽：    不用 [((笑))
29    光：         [((笑)) (        )
```

Compared with the above two examples, the request turn in this extracts is designed more delicately. Having registered receipt of the information, Guang (光) makes an "offer" to check the laptop's hardware for Li, preceded by a pro-forma "pre-offer" (Line 25). Although the surface benefit to Li is conveyed by a canonical offer format ("I will help you …"), there is no difficulty in identifying Guang as the actual beneficiary of this action. Common knowledge tells us that it is unnecessary to test performance of a new laptop. Instead of selecting the verb of "check" or "test", the use of the verb *play* ("玩儿玩儿") in a VV form downgrades the seriousness of the matter and the degree of the action, and inversely indexes a flavor that he will get benefit from his "offer". The benefactive stance (Clayman & Heritage, 2014) conveyed in the turn design is contrary to the actual benefactive status (ibid.) of his action. That is, Guang's "offer" indexes a reversed distribution of benefits and costs. Thus, Guang's action is a request camouflaged as an offer. The maneuver of designing a request in the guise of an offer displays that the requester is doing delicacy while initiating the request.

Ex. 13 [MA 14/TY/7：0：00]

(This conversation is called from Hui at the dormitory to her roommate Yu who is studying at the library.)

```
01    慧：    喂？hhh.
02    雨：    °怎么[了-°
03    慧：        [喂，田雨？=
04    雨：    =哎=
05    慧：    =你在图书馆了:?=
06    雨：    =嗯:在了,
07            (0.4)
08    慧：    咱们去吃饭吧?((笑))=
09    雨：    =你饿啦？
10            (0.5)
11    慧：    嗯:没- 我没有饿,但是我瞌睡得不行((笑))
12    雨：    行嘞, .hhh 那我那个:.hhh 那我就在那个,(0.4)
13            呃:餐厅门口等着你.((杂音))
14            (1.1)
15    慧：    嗯::行呢,
```

This example involves a proposal-framed request (Line 08). Here Hui (慧) and Yu (雨) are roommates. Hui calls to Yu to ask her to have lunch

CHAPTER FIVE DELICACY IN TURN DESIGN OF REQUESTING

through a canonical proposal format ("Let's..."). However, the underlying self-interested nature of the request can be unveiled by Yu's inquiry ("Are you hungry?") (Line 09). Her inquiry is not an innocent one but solicits an account indicating that it might be too early to have lunch, which is evidenced in Hui's response (Line 11). One can notice that Yu is occupied with studying at the library. Hui's request involves a departure from what Yu is doing now, which costs more on Yu. And her laughter (Line 11) may be hearable as a delicate acknowledgement of this concern. Here it turns out that Hui is the beneficiary of the proposal-framed request in that the aim of her proposal is to dispel sleepiness (Line 11). Here by camouflaging a request as a proposal, Hui tacitly eliminates costs of requesting to Yu and increases the possibility of granting of her request as well.

The above two examples demonstrate how requesters design their request turns subtly. By exploiting the distribution of benefits and/or costs, requesters deliver requesting in the guise of other actions. In this way, the request in the process of being delivered is detoxified with minimal portrayal of requesting.

5.4.2 Minimization of costs of requesting to requestees

Minimization of costs of requesting to requestees is often achieved by selecting "softened" verbs or formatting the request as involving a minimal departure from requestees' routine (Clayman & Heritage, 2014).

5.4.2.1 Selection of "softened" verbs

One practice often employed by requesters to minimize costs of requesting is to select "softened" verbs to mitigate cost or burden associated with the request being initiated.

Ex. 14 [MA 14/DY/1:0:31]

13　艳：　　>别别别别< 小事一桩，何必客气，不吃饭((笑))=

14 丽：   =哎呀，那多不好意思［了呀，
15 艳：   ［嗯::没事.
16 丽：   那个:呃:::我其实是还有另外一件事情，
17   就是:我想看一下你的那个笔记.

A truncated version of Ex. 10 in Chapter Four is re-presented here. Notice that the verb *to read the notes* ("看") is selected instead of the verb *to borrow it* ("借") in the request proper (Line 17). According to the common sense that it takes less time or cost to read something than to borrow something, the verb "to read the notes" conveys minimal nature of Li's request (Clayman & Heritage, 2014), thereby indicating a less burden on or costs to granting the request.

Ex. 15 ［LS 16/PZD/1:0:11］
13 淑：   咋啦，
14 东：   呃:::hhh.(0.3)帮我个忙呗？
15 淑：   你要干啥了，
16 东：   啊我翻译完你帮我看一下hh.

A similar softened pattern is present in this extract. The verb *to revise* ("修改") is replaced by the verb *have a look* ("看一下") in the request turn (Line 16) to connote the brevity and easiness of the action being requested. In this way, the cost of the request is mitigated and the likelihood of granting is increased.

Both examples manifest requesters' efforts at minimizing costs of requesting to requestees and simultaneously index a benefactor-beneficiary relationship. By selection of "softened" verbs, requesters tacitly deal with the self-interested nature of requesting, thereby reflexively demonstrating construction of delicacy.

5.4.2.2 A minimal departure from requestees' routine

Another practice deployed by requesters to minimize costs of requesting is to format the request as involving a minimal departure from requestees'

CHAPTER FIVE DELICACY IN TURN DESIGN OF REQUESTING

routine.

Ex. 16 [MA 14/TY/2:0:00]
01 慧: 喂:?
02 雨: °怎么了?°
03 慧: 喂,小雨,你睡着了?
04 雨: 没有,我在-°我在图书馆呢°.
05 慧: 噢::你一会儿去吃饭帮我拿一下快递哇::?

In this example, requesting is produced after a sequence-closing third *oh* ("噢::") (Schegloff, 2007) (Line 05). Notice that by adding a when-adverbial clause "when you go for lunch", Hui (慧) conveys that both the package delivery service might be on the way to the canteen or near the canteen and what she is requesting is not a special trip to fetch her package. In this way, the requesting is framed as a minimal departure from the requestee's routine, indexing a lower cost to the requestee.

Ex. 17 [MA 14/WM/8:0:00]
01 梦: 喂:?
02   (1.1)
03 菲: 喂:?
04 梦: 嗯,干嘛呢,
05 菲: 睡觉吗?
06   (0.9)
07 梦: 躺着呢,干嘛呢,
08   (0.5)
09 菲: 嗯::你下午要是有空的话帮我去取一下快递吧.

This example is a clear illustration of how the requester deals with the interactionally produced delicacy. In this telephone conversation Fei (菲) asks Meng (梦) to fetch the postal parcel for her. Not having known Meng's availability, Fei produces a conditional request following a half second gap and turn initial delay *uhm* ("嗯::") (Line 09). The if-conditional not only

· 111 ·

displays the requester's orientation to the contingency projected by hedging responses to her pre-requests, but also refers to the contingency associated with granting the request. By the hypotheticality or conditionality contained in the if-conditional, the requester implicitly acknowledges an alternative, thereby hedging her request to some degree or minimalizing costs to the requestee. Furthermore, placed in the turn-initial position, the if-conditional shows the requestee that an expanded turn is upcoming and postpones the request proper (Taleghani-Nikazm, 2006).

In both examples, the when-adverbial clause and the if-conditional clause serve to minimize the anticipated inconvenience or expected costs in granting the request. Once again, requesters' wording displays how expressive caution is being used to produce and manage delicacy in designing the request turn.

5.4.3 Maximization of benefits of requesting to requesters

Although there is a tendency to minimize costs (and impositions) of requesting to (and on) requestees, in other cases, requesters strive to maximize the benefits of requesting by which granting of requesting would fulfill.

Ex. 18 [LS 16/WXT/1:0:00]

(Shu and Ting are roommates, and there is a canteen named as Jiaogong near their dormitory building.)

```
01   淑：    喂:?
02           (0.8)
03   婷：    诶,淑,你在哪儿呢?=
04   淑：    =诶,晓婷,我在宿舍呢,(0.4)怎么[了?
05   婷：                              [$呵hhh..hhh呵$
06           你你,你来那个食堂解救一下我=教工食堂.
```

CHAPTER FIVE   DELICACY IN TURN DESIGN OF REQUESTING

```
07            $.hhh 我把钱包落在那个:那个所里了$=
08            =我现在买饭钱也没有卡也$没有$((笑))
09            $呵呵$.hhh hhh. 我先用一下你的
10    淑：    哦:>好的好的好的<行.
```

After having known Shu（淑）is available, Ting（婷）delivers her request. It can be noticed that Ting's request is composed of multiple TCUs: turn initial delay（Line 05）, the request proper（Line 06）and accounts（Lines 07-09）. At a first sight, the selection of the verb *save*（"解救"）seems to be a departure from the way of minimizing costs of requesting to requestees. Actually, the verb "save", often used in emergencies, strengthens the degree of urgency of the request and maximizes benefits of requesting to the requester. At the same time, accounts are in the service of acknowledging Ting herself as the beneficiary and Shu as the benefactor while dealing with untowardness of requesting. In this way, the requester clearly shows her orientation to the benefit-cost relationship underlying the process of initiating requesting. Besides, speaking with laughter（Lines 07-09）may function to save the face of the requester. As mentioned by Jefferson（1985）and Adelsward（1989）, face-threats can be alleviated by the use of laughter. A similar maximizing pattern is also present in Ex. 19.

Ex. 19 [PZD 17/WPF/1:1:27]

(This extract is taken from a telephone conversation made by Fei to Dong for seeking information about grinders.)

```
51    飞：    >你们啥时候回来<.
52            (0.6)
53    东：    明天呗明天:(.)呃能能回去就回去了.
54    飞：    嗯::行呢行呢.来了我还(.)得- 叫你-
55            你得还得教我(.)教我一下那个:>硝态氮和铵态氮<
56            怎么测呢=我还不[会.((笑))
57    东：                   [嗯:: °行°
```

After the sequence-closing third ("嗯:: 行呢行呢"), Fei (飞) initiates a request containing a request proper and an account (Lines 54-56). Apart from when-adverbial clause *when you come back* ("来了"), perturbations (self-repair) and an account to mark the requesting as delicate, the verb *have to* ("得") also serves the same function. By using the verb *have to*, the requester, seemingly maximizing the magnitude of imposition on the requestee, instead, makes requesting an action that can be accomplished only by the requestee. Thus, it increases the likelihood of granting the requesting. Additionally, by self-repair, the repairable ("我还(.)得- 叫你-") is changed into the repaired ("你得还得教我"), by which the agency is changing. In this way, not only is the agent changed from *I* ("我") to *you* ("你"), but also the future action is changed accordingly from the directive to the request. Both ways fully and dynamically reveal Fei's orientation towards the construction of delicacy while issuing his request.

5.5 Lexical-syntactic Formats of Requesting

Requesting may be formulated with different lexical-syntactic formats in different languages. In English, it can be formulated as imperatives (e.g. Pass me the x.), interrogatives (e.g. Could/Would you do x? or I was wondering if you/I could do x?), declaratives (e.g. I need (you to do) x.) or the name of the requested object (Twenty Marlborough.) (Curl & Drew, 2008). The same is true for requesting in Chinese. Because the data of the present study is mainly from telephone conversations, the way of naming the requested object, which usually occurs in face-to-face interaction, is scarcely used. The following section will discuss how delicacy is constructed in and by these diverse formats.

CHAPTER FIVE DELICACY IN TURN DESIGN OF REQUESTING

5.5.1 Imperatives

Imperatives are normally modified by turn-final particles or rising intonation when deployed as a practice to initiate a request.

Ex. 20 [MA 15/XM/1: 0: 00]

01　丽：　喂?
02　　　　(0.6)
03　敏：　°喂? 咋啦?°
04　丽：　°呃, 你在图书馆了是不?°
05　　　　(0.5)
06　敏：　嗯:,
07　丽：　嗯:那个那啥. hh 呃:我们学校最近图书馆那个文献资源
08　　　　不能用=就是进>那个图书馆.hhh 然后<你们学校能
09　　　　不能那个免费下载那个知网呀:啥的资源了.
10　　　　(0.8)
11　敏：　可以,
12　丽：　噢:那你完了把你的账号给我一下哇?

The elongated *oh* ("噢:") in the falling tone registers receipt of the information that Li (丽) asked and ends the question-answer sequence, namely the pre-request. Having received the go-ahead response, Li delivers her request directly in the imperative format, claiming her entitlement to initiate the request (Line 12). The addition of particle *wa* ("哇") at the final position of the imperative is a common practice to attenuate the strength of imposition of requesting. And the rising intonation, indexing a kind of asking for Li's permission, also functions to mitigate the degree of imposition of requesting. One point cannot be neglected is that Li's request is accompanied with a *na*-preface (Line 12). Here the *na*-preface makes Li's requesting as a "routine next" (Heritage & Sorjonen, 1994) in a course of

· 115 ·

action or "procedural consequentiality" (Schegloff, 1991). In other words, what Li says is based on the positive response of Min (敏), if Min's response were negative; Li would possibly abort her request. By the tacit nature of *na*-preface, namely the embedment of requests into a series of actions as outcome triggered by the result of the prior talk, Li downgrades the cost of her request to Min and increases the likelihood of her request to be granted as well.

Ex. 21 [MA 14/YXR/4: 0: 00]
01　飞：　°喂，秀荣?°
02　荣：　燕飞?
03　飞：　°诶：°
04　荣：　°诶：：你去图- 你去食堂的时候给我带个饭吧?°
05　飞：　噢，行，我一会先回宿舍呀［我还是给你-

The when-adverbial clause is visible in this episode in which the request is to buy food for Rong (荣). Through the when-adverbial clause *when you go to the canteen* ("你去食堂的时候") (Line 04), Rong identifies the simplicity of granting her request than would have been the case if Fei (飞) were not going to the canteen, thus indexing a lower cost to Fei. Furthermore, the when-adverbial clause implicitly acknowledges a presumption[①] that Fei will do something that Rong has anticipated, by which Rong shows that she has known that there is no potential obstacle for preventing her request from being granted. The turn-final particle *ba* ("吧") plus the rising intonation similarly serve to downgrade the strength of imposition of the request.

As shown in Ex. 20 and Ex. 21, requesters' ways of constructing delicacy and designing their requests share a common feature that although there is no obstacle preventing their requests from being granted, they use the final particle plus rising intonation to weaken the degree of imposition of

---

① This presumption is based on the fact that Rong and Fei are roommates and Rong clearly knows Fei's daily routine. The softening voice shows that Rong knows that Fei is at the library, which is evidenced in Rong's repair.

CHAPTER FIVE DELICACY IN TURN DESIGN OF REQUESTING

their requests and to make the initiated action identified as a request instead of other directives.

5.5.2 Interrogatives

In the collected data, two kinds of interrogatives are frequently adopted by requesters to initiate a request: tag questions and *nengbuneng*-interrogatives, as displayed in Ex. 22 and Ex. 23 respectively.

Ex. 22 [DIG 14/TY/7:0:00]

(This conversation is a longer version of Ex. 13.)

```
01    惠：    喂? hhh.
02    雨：    °怎么［了-°
03    惠：         ［喂，小雨? =
04    雨：    = 哎 =
05    惠：    = 你在图书馆了:? =
06    雨：    = 嗯: 在了,
07           (0.4)
08    惠：    咱们去吃饭吧?((笑)) =
09    雨：    = 你饿啦?
10           (0.5)
11    惠：    嗯:没- 我没有饿，但是我瞌睡的不行((笑))
12    雨：    行嘞,.hhh 那我那个:.hhh 那我就在那个,(0.4) 呃:
13           餐厅门口等着你.((杂音))
14           (1.1)
15    惠：    嗯::行呢,
16    雨：    嗯:,.hhh 那个.hhh 你帮我带上餐具吧 = 装在一块儿
17           你帮我提着，行吧?
18    惠：    嗯:行呢.
```

After the proposal-like sequence (Lines 01-15), a request is initiated

· 117 ·

by an imperative plus a tag question. Here attention will be paid to the employment of the tag question. By the former imperative, a request can be clearly identified. Adding a tag question, the request proper gets expanded and specified. The tag which aims to ask for permission, functions to downgrade the strength of imposition of requesting on Hui (惠). It is not difficult to notice that from the turn design two parties are accustomed to going to the canteen with their own tableware. And the initiation of the request is subsequent to Hui's disguised proposal being accepted, when Hui is right at the dormitory. So it is easy and even obligatory for Hui to grant Yu's request, leaving no reason for rejection. Under such circumstances, Yu's request formulated by the imperative with the tag question explicitly inquires for Hui's permission, displaying requester's tacit management of the construction of her request.

Ex. 23 [DIG 17/HB/2:0:00]

01　冰：　喂,
02　　　　(0.6)
03　瑜：　韩冰呀.
04　冰：　嗯?
05　　　　(0.6)
06　瑜：　你在宿舍吗?
07　冰：　嗯:
08　　　　(0.7)
09　瑜：　你在干嘛? 在床上呢?
10　冰：　没有,(0.2) 电脑跟前了.
11　　　　(0.9)
12　瑜：　你能不能帮我收一下衣服=我今天回去就九点多啦.
13　　　　(1.3)
14　冰：　呃, 外边儿了?

In this telephone call Yu (瑜) employs the *A-not-A* question format,

CHAPTER FIVE   DELICACY IN TURN DESIGN OF REQUESTING

one type of disjunctive questions①, to formulate a laundry-collection request to Bing(冰), with an account latched at the TRP (Line 12). Here, the *nengbuneng*-interrogative displays Yu's orientation to whether Bing (冰) is able to grant her request. By the *nengbuneng*-interrogative, Yu downgrades the imposition of her request and provides Bing with the opportunity to opt out as well. That is, Bing has the opportunity to give a dispreferred response, rejection. Whatever be her reasons for it, the rejection could be formulated as due to her inability rather than unwillingness.

In the existing data, when requesting is implemented by interrogatives, *nengbuneng*-interrogatives are the major format deployed by requesters, while the tag question is scarcely used and only one case of the tag question is found. The former makes requesting appropriate and leaves room for requestees to opt out, while the latter shows requesting is treated with caution, which needs explicitly asking for the requestee's permission. The selection of interrogatives (to inquire about requestees' willingness or ability or to ask for requestees' permission to do requests) can be considered a milder alternative to imperatives, the default format, to deliver a request, which embodies requesters' delicate orientation toward their requesting.

5.5.3 Declaratives

Requesters normally employ *I want/say*-declaratives to deliver a request when there are possible obstacles preventing their requests from being granted.

---

① Disjunctive questions with or without the morpheme *haishi* "or" always present an either-or choice to the respondent. Two types of disjunctive questions exist. First, there are those composed of at least two constitutents connected by *haishi* "or". The second category of disjunctive questions consists of an affirmative sentence followed by its negative counterpart, usually without *haishi* "or". This type of question is traditionally called the *A-not-A* question, where "not" stands for one of the negative particles *bu* or *mei* (*you*) (Li & Thompson, 1989: 531-532).

Ex. 24 ［PZD 17/WH/4：0：00］

01　翰：　°东哥°

02　东：　诶阿↑翰↓::hh.

03　翰：　啊, hh.

04　　　　(0.3)

05　东：　呃::［在哪儿呢 hh.

06　翰：　　［(°>怎么啦<°)

07　　　　(0.5)

08　翰：　((杂音))我在四楼咋啦?

09　　　　(0.5)

10　东：　哎::.hh 我(.)想用一下你的那个: hh.(0.7)离心机么.

11　　　　(0.6)

12　翰：　啊:那:那那个你用就行了我- 我这会儿就下来了你用呗.

Having learned Han's (翰) whereabouts (Lines 05-08), Dong (东) infers that Han might be currently unavailable which is evidenced by the elongated *ai* ("哎::") in a disappointed tone. Given the current circumstance that Han is not fully available, Dong embeds his request within the statement of his thought (Line 10). By the *I want*-declarative, what Dong is doing is merely reporting his need or what his thought was when encountering trouble. In this way, it shows Dong's concern about not imposing on Han and it gives Han an opportunity to volunteer the help, thereby avoiding putting Han in a position of having to grant or reject an explicit request.

Ex. 25 ［DIG 16/ZJ/1：0：00］

01　淑：　喂:? 咋了, 美女,

02　　　　(0.9)

03　静：　喂:?

04　淑：　诶,

05　　　　(1.0)

06　静：　你在不在学校了:

CHAPTER FIVE　DELICACY IN TURN DESIGN OF REQUESTING

07　淑：　我在呢呀？怎么啦？
08　静：　嗯:上自习还是干嘛了.
09　淑：　我准备吃饭了这会儿hhh.
10　　　　(1.2)
11　静：　准备吃饭了:=
12　淑：　=嗯,你有事儿呢:?=
13　静：　=在文瀛？
14　淑：　我[还没过去呢,
15　静：　　[(还是-)
16　静：　还是令德了.
17　淑：　还没[过去hhh.-
18　静：　　　[嗯,我- 我拿的- 我拿好多东西我回不去了,
19　　　　我说让你过来,(.)我放你-((笑))放你后面,
20　　　　((笑))
21　淑：　噢:[行,行行行,你在哪儿呢？

Here, the inference that the requestee Shu (淑) might be unavailable to grant Jing's request can be made from the lengthy pre-requests (Lines 06-07, 08-09, 13-17). In such a case, similar to Ex. 24, Jing's request is also packaged in report of one's thought or need in the *I say*-declarative, showing that Jing is in a state of needing one's help, which increases the likelihood of requesting to be granted to some degree. Thanks to this format, the requestee is left with space to respond at her will on the one hand, and she may feel that she should grant the request in the moral sense on the other. This is a well-tuned way to initiate a request.

Based on the above analysis, it can be noticed that impositions of requesting indexed in imperatives, interrogatives and declaratives show a downward trend. But delicacy of requesting displayed in these lexical-syntactic formats is not only manifested in the minimized impositions and the conditional relevant constraint of FPPs on SPPs accordingly, but also in the very choice of one format instead of other alternatives. The entitlement of making the request and the contingency of the request being granted are delicately managed and displayed in and through the choice of lexical-syntactic formats to do requests.

5.6　Summary

The present chapter focuses on the aspect of constructing delicacy in turn designs of requesting. It has demonstrated that there are mainly five ways deployed to mark the request turn as delicate: deferring the request, packaging accounts, providing appreciation, indexing a distribution of benefits and/or costs associated with requesting and diverse lexical-syntactic formats of requesting. These practices clearly show requesters' expressive caution in initiating requesting.

As reviewed in Chapter Two, turn initial delay and perturbations are delicacy-markers used to display delicacy. The present observation also further substantiates their functions. Prefacing a request with other actions is another practice to defer the initiation of requesting objectively. By packaging accounts in the request turn, requesters manage the untowardness of requesting and account for the face-threatening act, thereby showing how delicacy is made visible in designing the request turn and implicitly acknowledging a benefit-cost relationship. This relationship can also be acknowledged in providing appreciation, which has the function of offsetting requestees' costs to some extent.

Regarding the benefit-cost relationship, it is fundamentally linked to the way of indexing a distribution of benefits and/or costs associated with requesting, which can be categorized into three types: minimal portrayal of requesting, minimization of costs of requesting to requestees and maximization of benefits of requesting to requesters. These practices mobilized in turn management

CHAPTER FIVE DELICACY IN TURN DESIGN OF REQUESTING

mainly display how benefits and costs to requesters and requestees respectively are embodied and balanced.

In terms of different lexical-syntactic formats of requesting, imperatives, interrogatives and declaratives are utilized to demonstrate how intrinsic imposition of requesting on requestees is dealt with. Through these formats, requesters show that when asking for help, they are normally sensitive to the degree to which they are imposing on requestees. And simultaneously, they attempt to minimize the anticipated inconvenience or expected impositions, avoiding having requestees pay too much and ensuring that they have alternatives way out. As the foregoing analysis demonstrates, it is visible that different syntactic formats used to initiate requesting are not interchangeable. The reason why one format is selected to produce a request when other alternatives are available will be explicated in the next chapter.

It is the above practices utilized in the turn design of requesting that provide analysts with evidences to expose how delicacy is constructed in requesting and how requesting is subtly treated. The adjustment of presentation of the imposition, costs and benefits is a display of requesters' orientation to delicacy of requesting in turn designs. So far, it has been illustrated what the delicate features in requesting are in both sequence organization (in Chapter Four) and turn design (in this chapter). That is, what is done in and through turns at talk is demonstrated and how it is done or constructed is also presented. But the question of why requesting is initiated and managed in the way it is – what is achieved by doing so? why is it done in these ways? and what drives it done so? – remains untouched. The answer will be found in the next chapter.

CHAPTER SIX   THE DELICACY OF REQUESTING AND SOCIAL SOLIDARITY

6.1   Introduction

As the present study is concerned with the delicacy of requesting, the prior two chapters made a close observation of how the delicacy of requesting is constructed in requesting sequences and turn designs respectively. However, the focus of the study is not only on the description of the delicacy of requesting and its construction and management, but also on the question of why it is constructed and managed in the way it is – what is achieved by doing this?

6.1.1   Altruism

This subsection begins by introducing what altruism is, especially the definition of altruism in this study. The term "altruism" is coined by the French sociologist and positivist Auguste Comte (1798-1857). As a contrast to egoism, altruism is defined as an unselfish desire to live for others (Comte, 1851; cf: Post, 2014; Wilson, 2015). It is the foundation of all social relations and morality (Comte, 1851; cf: Post, 2014). A thorough review of extensive literature on altruism reveals that studies on altruism

CHAPTER SIX　THE DELICACY OF REQUESTING AND SOCIAL SOLIDARITY

mainly focus on the following questions: What is altruism? Does altruism exist? And if it does, what are the roots of altruism? These questions are mainly distributed in biology, economics and psychology, etc. However, there is no general consensus on these questions. As for the definition of altruism, scholars from different disciplines conceptualize it differently. Oliner and Oliner (1988) belong to the scholars who define altruism only from the perspective of behavior. They propose that a behavior can be defined as altruistic when (1) it is directed toward helping another, (2) it involves high risk or sacrifice to the actor, (3) it is accompanied by no external reward and (4) it is voluntary (Oliner & Oliner, 1988: 6). Instead some scholars propose that altruism is not a property of behavior and it should be defined in terms of individuals' motivations: altruism is a motivational state with the ultimate goal of increasing another's welfare (Batson, 1991: 6). Still others, defining altruism, focus on both behavior and motivation. For example, Macaulay and Berkowitz (1970) define altruism as behavior carried out without the anticipation of rewards from external sources (1970: 3). Tellingly, other-directed, costly helping and welfare are three key words in different versions of the definition of altruism. In other words, the essence in definitions of altruism is that of benefiting the welfare of others in different ways costly to the actor.

　　Wilson's definition is a preferred version in this study. Altruism is a concern for the welfare of others as an end in itself. Improving the welfare of others often requires a cost in terms of time, energy, and risk. Even the simple act of opening a door for someone requires a tiny expenditure of time and energy. At the opposite extreme, saving a life often requires a substantial risk to one's own (Wilson, 2015: 3). But it would be wrong to accept it uncritically. Questions arise: how do we observe and measure motivation objectively? Is the altruistic behavior always beneficial to recipients? For example, is it still beneficial to others when they are not in need? Is altruism restricted to material resources or forces? Based on these prior works, the definition of altruism in this study is somewhat broadened: actions are designed to benefit recipients materially and spiritually, even at the risk of harm to actors' own welfare. An action can be characterized as altruistic when (1)it is voluntary, (2)it is directed toward showing considerateness to the recipient and (3) it involves sacrifice to the actor, which includes involvement of mitigating the recipient's possible cost or effort to do something. In the meantime, it is worthy of mentioning that an altruistic action possibly getting rewards or benefits cannot be excluded from the term of altruism. The reason why is that the existence of a helpful act, no matter how heroic or risky, does not rule out the possibility that benefiting the other was only an instrumental means to reach the ultimate goal of benefiting onself (Batson, 2011: 88-89).

6.1.2 Social norms

The term "social norms" has been extensively studied in many different disciplines. Anthropologists have explored the role played by social norms in different cultures (Geertz, 1973), economists have focused on influences on market behavior resulting from conformity to social norms (Akerlof, 1976; Young, 1998) and even legal scholars have described how social norms function as backups to legal rules (Ellickson, 1991; Posner, 2000), etc. But in sociology, much attention has been paid to social functions social norms perform (Parsons, 1937; Durkheim, 1950; Parsons & Shils, 1951; Hechter & Opp, 2001), accounts of why social norms exist (Akerlof, 1976; Ullmann-Margalit, 1977), and analysis of conditions under which social norms come into being (Axelrod, 1986; Skyrms, 1996). As for the definitions of social norms, it has been defined in many different ways. For example, there is a general definition of social norms: principles or models

CHAPTER SIX THE DELICACY OF REQUESTING AND SOCIAL SOLIDARITY

of behavior specific to a given social group or society. Social norms are in keeping with what is commonly accepted and legitimized by the value system specific to each society or social group (Alpe, Lambert, Beitone, Dollo & Parayre, 2007: 204). By Durkheimian analysis, social norms are defined as social facts: manners of acting, thinking, and feeling external to the individual, which are invested with a coercive power by virtue of which they exercise control over him (Durkheim, 1895, cf: Revillard, 2019). This study adopts Popitz's definition of social norms – norms as those expected forms of regular behavior whose absence or violation causes social sanctions (Popitz, 2017: 3). According to Popitz (2017), people know of a norm when they expect sanctions as a result of its violation, or when they react to other people's violations with sanctions. In a simple case, a violation of a norm is followed by a negative reaction. As a consequence, the norm is kept intact and the social order in question is stabilized (Popitz, 2017: 3). In other words, social norms are not laws. They cannot be breached and norms are enforced by sanctions.

How do social norms come to be understood thoroughly? The answer should be made from the following three aspects: conformity to and violation of social norms, and consequences resulting from violation of social norms as well. Suppose when you ask your friend a question what expectation do you have? Your expectation will be that your question gets an answer, which is preferred over a response "I don't know". But when there is non-occurrence of an answer or a response, what will you do then? You might account for why s/he did not answer. For example, maybe s/he does not know, maybe s/he did not hear your question, maybe your question is not appropriate or s/he does not like to answer. Or you might ask the question once more or you might ask directly why s/he did not answer. The possible accounts that you make or the potential action you will do is the evidence that you noticed the missing behavior – a response from your friend. In other words, when the question-answer norm is violated, the questioner's subsequent conduct such as pursuit, inference and report (Sidnell, 2010), is the best evidence of her/his orientation to the answerer's violation of the norm. Here are two examples to illustrate how social norms play a role in our interaction.

Ex. 1 (cite from Drew, 1981: 249)

```
01 Mother:   What's the time- by the clock?
02 Roger:    Uh
03 Mother:   What's the time?
04           (3.0)
05 Mother:   (Now) what number's that?
06 Roger:    Number two
07 Mother:   No it's not
08           What is it?
09 Roger:    It's a one and a nought
```

After her question (Line 01) is met with a voice of "Uh" (which is noticeable absence of an answer) (Line 02), the mother asks again the question in an abbreviated form (Line 03). Orienting to the missing answer (Line 04), mother asks the question in a straightforward way (Line 05), which gets an answer (Line 06). The normative character of a question – when a question is asked, an answer should be volunteered next – is displayed in the mother's pursuits of a response twice due to Roger's failure to answer and Roger's production of an answer. That is, the questioner is entitled to get an answer once the norm is violated. Consider the following example, in which account is provided for failure to answer.

Ex. 2 (cited from Heritage, 1988: 133)

```
01 J: But the trai:n goes. Does th'train go o:n
02    th'boa:t?
03 M: .h .h Ooh I've no idea:. She ha: sn't sai:d.
```

M responds with a disclaimer, ("I've no idea") which is followed by an

CHAPTER SIX THE DELICACY OF REQUESTING AND SOCIAL SOLIDARITY

account. By reference to the third party, M clearly accounts for her inability, namely, she is not unwilling to provide an answer but she is unable to, because the answer to J's question belongs to the epistemic domain of the third party. Here M's account displays her orientation to the failure to answer J's question or to her departure from the norm. This is also evidence that the role the norm plays, that is, the normative expectation is set up when a question is asked. The above two examples have illustrated that when social norms are conformed, no special attention will be paid to. But when there is a departure from social norms, it will be noticed, sanctioned or even incurred morally negative assessment①. Based on the understanding of social norms, the following Sections 6.3 will display how requesters' orientation to social norms is bound to requesting.

6.1.3 Social solidarity

Research on issues of social solidarity has roughly gone through three stages (namely, from the latter part of the nineteenth century, to the era of Durkheim and to present-day modernity) since its origins (Tiryakian & Morgan, 2014). The concept of "solidarity" in the West is rooted in legal terminology, going back at least to Roman law (Bierhoff, 2002: 281), in which it was used to identify shared or collective liability by members of the same extended family, or "Gens" (Smith & Sorrell, 2014: 222). Broad as it is, issues of solidarity involve in the cultural, legal, political, ethical and social affairs, etc., which will not be discussed in details for the theme of the present study. The importance of the concept of solidarity is indebted to one of the most crucial sociologists, the French sociologist Emile Durkheim, who proposes two types of solidarity: mechanical and organic solidarity in his

---

① Garfinkel's breaching experiments (1967) could serve as a glamor evidence for this conclusion.

dissertation *The Division of Labor in Society* published in 1893. This book was "translated" by Talcott Parsons into English in his book *The Structure of Social Action* in 1937. Because of the strong influence of these two books, the key concept of "solidarity" that social scientists use today most obviously comes into the English-speaking world from Durkheim through Parsons, and thus carries with it some of the concerns embedded in the history of the use of that idea in France in the second half of the nineteenth century (Smith & Sorrell, 2014: 225).

Although their books play key roles in understanding what solidarity is, different social-science disciplines and explanatory paradigms such as rational-choice theorists, functionalism and evolutionary psychology, etc. have offered divergent interpretation of solidarity. Often discussed with concepts like group, unity, or social cohesion, solidarity is described as any kind of bond that holds a group or community together; usually, however, authors specify solidarity as a particular kind of bond holding a group together, especially the glue of identity, or an active identification of oneself as a part of a group in a way that implies an investment of some nature in the group (Cureton, 2012; Foote, 1951; Melucci, 1996; Smith & Sorrell, 2014: 227). In this way, solidarity also carries the implication of some sort of unity with group or of a sense that the members of the group share something and have a stake in its well-being (Cureton, 2012; Scholz, 2008; Smith & Sorrell, 2014: 228). Simultaneously some scholars (Blumer, 1939; Hunt, 1991; Scholz, 2008) define solidarity on the basis of an affective dimension, while others, from the perspective of a normative dimension, discuss that solidary relationships are based on shared values or norms (Bayertz, 1999; Cureton, 2012; Smith & Sorrell, 2014: 228). Based on these different definitions, it can be noticed that solidarity is multidimensional. It is difficult to make a definition of this concept without missing the complex ways that solidarity works within social life.

CHAPTER SIX THE DELICACY OF REQUESTING AND SOCIAL SOLIDARITY

In the present study, the working definition of solidarity adopts Yu's (2010): solidarity is a dynamic achievement in verbal communication, and solidarity could be established by various communicative strategies. Taking its dynamic feature into consideration, solidarity can be established, maintained or destroyed (Yu, 2010: 229-230).

6.2 Altruism and Social Solidarity

In this section the relationship between altruism and social solidarity will be considered. It aims to unravel how, at first glance, the seemingly insignificant details in requesting sequences and turn designs of requesting are deployed for displaying other-attentiveness or showing other concerns and to explore what the interactional implications of these different ways in which altruism is exquisitely displayed are.

6.2.1 Altruism in requesting sequences

As demonstrated in Chapter Four, delicacy in requesting, in terms of sequence organization, is normally constructed by pre-sequences, especially by pre-requests. Pre-requests, one of the normative practices used when requesting is launched, demonstrate the requester's altruistic orientation, despite the self-interested nature of requesting.

6.2.1.1 Altruism in pre-requests

The initiation of requesting is normally accompanied with pre-requests. The following analysis will show that pre-requests are deployed to accomplish other-attentive course of action – showing concerns for the requestee, thereby exposing the requester's interest in the requestee and downplaying the self-interested nature of the request.

Ex. 3 [MA 14/SH/9:0:00]

(Liu and Shi, who are both classmates and roommates, usually have dinner at a canteen called Lingde, near which there is a Package Delivery Service.)

01　柳：　吃饭没，
02　石：　没呢.
03　　　　(1.0)
04　柳：　去不去了.
05　石：　去了呀？
06　柳：　去令德了？
07　石：　哦，那去哪儿呀，
08　柳：　取个：(.)包裹呗.

In this example, the pre-requests (Lines 01-07), consisting of three question-answer adjacency pairs (Lines 01-02, 04-05 & 06-07), mainly deal with the requestee's life-world. Throughout the pre-requests Liu (柳) clearly shows concern for Shi (石) as evidenced by the way he designs his three questions. His first question suggests that the call was made around the dinnertime in that questions like whether you have dinner or not are normally not asked when it's not dinnertime. And common knowledge tells us that the possible answer is yes, no or being having dinner. Shi's negative answer, not-yet having dinner (Line 02), paves the path for Liu to ask whether Shi is still going to dinner (Line 04). (Otherwise, if Shi's answer were yes, the trajectory of the conversation might be changed and the request might be abandoned, while if Shi's answer were that he was having dinner, the canteen where he was should be the focus of the following conversation.) Liu's second question is also other-attentive for it concerns Shi's plan about whether he is going to dinner and not having had dinner yet may not be a necessary signal that Shi must or will go. Here, if the answer were a negative one, the trajectory of the conversation also might be changed and the request might be

CHAPTER SIX THE DELICACY OF REQUESTING AND SOCIAL SOLIDARITY

abandoned as well. But the positive answer (Line 05) opens another door for Liu's third question checking whether Shi is going to the same canteen as usual (the point is this canteen is near the Package Delivery Service) (Line 06). The third question is another other-attentive inquiry concerning Shi's plan about the canteen where he is going to for dinner. The design of his question in a declarative format with a question tone suggests that Liu is highly familiar with Shi, indexing their ongoing social relationship (Sigman, 1995). At the point of his checking being confirmed (Line 07), Liu rushes into launching his request directly in the imperative format (Line 08). This example displays the carefully organized local trajectory of assessing the contingency and entitlement of a request, which will be discussed in Section 6.3.

The pre-requests and the very position of initiation of the request provide support for understanding the requester's altruistic stance or other-attentiveness. As is presented the pre-requests address the requestee-regarding matters. It is obvious to see that the pre-requests, centering on the requestee, show that the requester is fundamentally estimating the cost of the possible request to the requestee in a progressive way. Not until the possible request being a relatively low cost action has been confirmed does the requester Liu deliver his request. This kind of concern for others mainly involving the requester's attempt to check the cost of her/his request to the requestee or to make sure that her/his request is minimally burdensome to the requestee is also presented in the following example.

Ex. 4 [MA 14/SH/8:0:00]

(Shi and Mei are classmates.)

```
01    石：   喂？
02           (1.2)
03    梅：   喂,你在哪儿呢？
04    石：   我在:我:么:呃::旧楼.
05           (1.0)
```

```
06   梅：    你中午在哪儿吃饭呀.
07   石：    中午在哪儿吃饭？咋了么你要.
08          (0.7)
09   梅：    哦：我就说吧，你给我去那个令德超市＝就是那个原来
10          移动的营业厅那儿(.)取个圆通的快递吧＝我回家啦.
11          (0.5)
12   石：    嗯：行，
```

In this example, the caller Mei（梅）also launches a requestee-attentive course of action dealing with the requestee-regarding matters by pre-requests（Lines 03-07）. At Line 03, Mei's question is an other-attentive inquiry about Shi's whereabouts. After the answer（Line 04）followed by a gap（Line 05）comes Mei's another other-attentive question about Shi's plan concerning the canteen where he is going to have lunch（Line 06）. Instead of producing an answer, subsequent to the repetition of Mei's question, Shi（石）asks the reason for Mei's question（Line 07）, which is also the reason for the call. Nothing else is immediately brought up and a gap develops（Line 08）. Note first Mei's response at Lines 09-10 addresses double faceted constraints by Shi's question format and action. The former part, *Okay. Then, I will say it*（"哦：我就说吧"）, registers receipt of the information conveyed by Shi's question and further projects an answer to be provided. And the latter part, the request plus an account, not only answers the question but also responds to the action forwarding the sequence to the base FPP. Note, then, that the *Okay. Then, I will say it*（"哦：我就说吧"）, serves to mark a shift in the center of the conversation from Shi to Mei herself. This shift, made in response to Shi, provides data-internal evidence（Schegloff, 2007）that the requester herself demonstrably is the requestee-centered from incipiency.

Similar to Ex 3, the requester assesses the cost of her request to the requestee in and through pre-requests. As discussed in Section 4.1, pre-

CHAPTER SIX THE DELICACY OF REQUESTING AND SOCIAL SOLIDARITY

requests are used to check the requestee's availability or to explore whether there are obstacles for the requestee to grant the request. According to our common knowledge, normally the more obstacles there are, the more costly the request is for the requestee all else being equal. This is strongly consistent with the current observations that a request is overwhelmingly initiated when pre-requests are not blocked. In other words, a request is not initiated until it is estimated as a relatively low cost action to the requestee. Taken together, it suggests that the requester shows concern for the requestee and conveys an altruistic stance in and through pre-requests. Although requesting intrinsically benefits the requester rather than the requestee, a request is normally initiated after the requester has ensured that the requested object or service does not cost much to the requestee. If it is not so, the request would usually be abandoned. Perhaps, such an altruistic stance can be best demonstrated in cases where pre-requests get blocked.

Ex. 5 [PZD 17/WH/3: 0: 00]
(Dong and Han are roommates and classmates.)

```
01          (0.5)
02   东:   喂,
03          (0.8)
04   翰:   喂:东哥,
05   东:   诶.
06          (0.5)
07   翰:   呃你那个:这会方便着没, (0.2) 你在外面吃饭着没,
08   东:   没有h.
09          (0.3)
10   东:   我[在宿舍呢现在.
11   翰:     [哦你还在实验吗-
12          (0.8)
13   翰:   ang:好吧那[我-
```

14	东:	［嗯＝
15	翰:	＝行吧那那（0.5）那行吧.
16		(0.3)
17	东:	怎么了？
18		(0.4)
19	翰:	诶我我-((笑))＄快递有点多＄我说.h 我以为你出
20		来吃饭我说你帮我(.)去(.)提一下么是哇,

Before initiating a request, similarly to the above examples, the requester Han (翰) "prepares the field" with pre-requests (Lines 02-10). The successive two questions about the requestee Dong's (东) availability at Line 07 are designed from general to specific. After the negative answer (Line 08), there is a 0.3 second gap. Due to this gap, Dong and Han starts their turn almost at the same time and there is an overlap between Lines 10 and 11. Dong volunteers his whereabouts (Line 10), suggesting that Han's prior questions have been understood as preliminary to something else. Overlapping with Dong's turn, Han seeks confirmation about Dong's current location (Line 11), which is simultaneously disconfirmed by Dong's turn (Line 10). Note that Han proceeds with two tokens of sequence-closing thirds (Schegloff, 2007). The elongated *ang* is in the service of information-registering; the *okay* ("好吧") functions to accept Dong's blocking response to his pre-requests on the one hand and to show Dong's response is out of his expectation on the other (Wu Yaxin & Yang Yongfang, 2019). At Line 15 Han re-deploys sequence-closing thirds projecting both a possible sequence-closing and abandonment of the action projected by the pre-sequences. The abandoned action turns out to be a request after Dong's pursuit (Line 17), which shows Dong's understanding of the previous turns as preliminary to certain further actions. Han's abandonment of the request displays his consideration of Dong's whereabouts or convenience prior to delivering the request, which is the evidence of altruistic thinking in doing requests.

CHAPTER SIX   THE DELICACY OF REQUESTING AND SOCIAL SOLIDARITY

6.2.2   Altruism in turn designs of requesting

When it comes to the phase of initiating a request, the request is normally formatted as not self-interested alone, rather other-interested and somewhat altruistic. Such other-interested and altruistic laminations are presented in three aspects: minimal portrayal of the possible cost of the request, minimization of the possible cost to the requestee's granting and offset/balance of the cost to the requestee by providing benefits as appreciations.

6.2.2.1   Minimal portrayal of the possible cost of the request

In some cases, a request may be formulated as minimal cost to or imposition on the requestee by a selective group of verbs (or verb phrases). Such a choice of verbs or verb phrases is usually designed to connote the brevity or ease of the action being requested when it is performed or the least, if possible, involvement with the object being requested.

Ex. 6 [LS 16/PZD/1:0:11]

```
01  东：  [喂,
02  淑：  [( )
03        (0.2)
04  淑：  诶,
05        (0.8)
06  东：  美女(0.2)((轻声笑))
07  淑：  咋:啦:
08  东：  ((笑))忙不忙呀 hhh.?
09        (0.6)
10  淑：  咋啦?
11        (0.6)
12  东：  嗯?
```

13	淑：	咋啦，
14	东：	呃::hhh.(0.3)帮我个忙呗?
15	淑：	你要干啥了，
16	东：	我翻译完你帮我看一下hh.
17	淑：	$呵呵$

This extract is the replication of Ex. 15 in Chapter Five. It is noticeable that Dong（东）frames his request in the imperative with assurance of brevity by *have a look*（"看一下"）（Line 16）. Instead of *revising* or *reviewing*, which is more complicated and time-consuming, just *having a look* communicates the sense of brevity in doing the requested thing, indexing a low cost and ease of the requested action. Thus a minimal nature of one's request （Clayman & Heritage, 2014）is conveyed and accordingly the likelihood of granting is increased. And a similar case is presented in the following conversation. In Ex. 7, Li calls to borrow Yan's notebook.

Ex. 7 [MA 14/DY/1:0:31]

12	丽：	=那:我想:咱们:请你吃个饭，
13	艳：	>别别别别< 小事一桩，何必客气，不吃饭((笑))=
14	丽：	=哎呀，那多不好意思[了呀，
15	艳：	[嗯::没事.
16	丽：	那个:呃::我其实是还有另外一件事情，
17		就是:我想看一下你的那个笔记.

A truncated version of Ex. 10 in Chapter Four is re-presented here. Note that Li's choice of the verb *to read the notes*（"看"）, instead of the verb *to borrow it*（"借"）is accompanied with the declarative to construct her request（Line 17）. Here Li uses *to read* to characterize her minimal involvement with the requestee's object: it will take her only a short time to keep the notebook and she will return it soon, thereby connoting a minimal cost of the request and in tandem increasing the likelihood of granting the request. In addition, in this case, the choice of the declarative format may be influenced

CHAPTER SIX THE DELICACY OF REQUESTING AND SOCIAL SOLIDARITY

by the blocked going-in-front-of requests: her invitation both as appreciation for Yan's previous help and as a wedge for the initiation of the upcoming request is rejected. It is visible that the cautious beginning of the request turn "actually I have another thing to bring up" (Line 16) seizes the floor[①], successfully making the transition from ending the current goal of showing appreciation to introducing the primary goal. Here, the declarative format, indexing the low entitlement and high contingency to initiate the request, is also another way to mark the minimal nature of the request, for the declarative, as the FPP, does not set strictly conditionally relevant constraint on the SPP.

6.2.2.2 Minimization of the possible cost to the requestee's granting

In other cases, a request may be formulated as minimal interference with the requestee's routine life, which is clearly illustrated below.

Ex. 8 [PZD 18/ZXB/1:0:00]

(Biao and Dong are colleagues. Dong who is currently studying an in-service postgraduate program in another city calls Biao to ask him to fetch his package.)

```
01          (0.7)
02   东：  [诶.
03   彪：  [(诶.)
04          (1.7)
05   彪：  喂.
06   东：  喂. 在哪呢,
07          (1.6)
08   彪：  在家么怎么啦?
```

---

① Yan's rejection to Li's invitation closes the sequence-so-far and a possible sequence completion is brought to a possible close. At this point by the turn initial delay *nage*: ("那个:") and the filler *e*: ("呃:") and the employment of *actually* ("其实"), Li takes the opportunity to expand the sequence. Otherwise, if this opportunity were missed, the sequence would get closed by Li's acceptance of Yan's rejection.

09   (0.4)
10 东： 诶你：那啥(.)你下去的时候到门房拿一下我的快递吧.

Having confirmed that Biao（彪）is available, Dong（东）delivers his request preceded by a when-adverbial clause "when you go out" (Line 10). The addition of this clause displays that his request is not urgent, does not require a special trip and does not specify the exact time to fulfill his request. In this way, Dong's effort to minimize the possible cost (or imposition) of his requested action to (or on) the requestee is conveyed – A similar minimizing pattern can also be found in Ex. 16 in Chapter Five, which will not be discussed in detail. In both examples, the initiated requests can be fulfilled during the requestees' trip to the destination, which displays minimal interference with the requestee's routines, thereby reducing the cost to or imposition on the requestee.

Ex. 9 [MA 14/ZXF/2:0:00]
01 美： 小白？=
02 白： =喂？嗯.(0.3)咋了.=
03 美： =等会还来不来啦.
04   (1.2)
05 白： 去哪呀,
06 美： 那个你们办公室.
07   (1.4)
08 白： 你找我啦？
09 美： 你去不去么=
10   =你要是去就给我- 帮我把硬盘拿过来.
11   (1.5)
12 白： 硬盘？

This case, similar to Ex. 17 in Chapter Five, is another exquisite demonstration of the requester's awareness of minimizing the cost of the upcoming request to the requestee or the requester's altruistic stance when

CHAPTER SIX THE DELICACY OF REQUESTING AND SOCIAL SOLIDARITY

initiating her request. With a lack of certainty about whether Bai (白) will go to her office, Mei produces a pro-forma confirmation-seeking (Line 09) after which her request is initiated subsequent to an if-conditional clause (Line 10). The use of "If you will go" displays that Mei is not only assessing Bai's cost to be paid for granting her request but also tries to minimize the possible cost. In the meantime, Mei provides an opportunity for Bai to reject the request with both parties' face unimpaired. That is, if Bai's response were rejection, it would be a negation to the if-conditional clause instead of the request proper. Thus, the imposition of the request on the requestee is also reduced. In this way, Mei shows two-sided concern for Bai: both moderating the cost to the requestee's granting of her request and putting herself in the other's shoes.

6.2.2.3 Balance of the cost to the requestee by providing benefits

There is still one case in which the requester uses benefits-provision as a way to balance the possible cost of his request to the requestee as shown in the example below.

Ex. 10 [MA 11/LL/1:0:44]

```
15        (3.3)
16    明：要不下次你::我卖的时候你指导指导我在我身边,
17        (1.1)
18    明：(  ) 我请你吃饭?
19    博：哦, 没事, 下回你就- >你跟的你跟的<
20        你这两天看的就行了.
```

In the prior conversation, Bo provides advice twice as solutions to Ming's trouble. After the long gap (Line 15), Ming, instead of giving a response to the preceding advice (cf. Ex. 8 in Chapter Four), initiates his request followed by a gap (Line 17) which is a possible harbinger of forthcoming rejection (Schegloff, 2007). In the face of the possibility of a rejection, Ming offers an invitation (Line 18), getting the request turn

· 141 ·

expanded and functioning as both compensation for Bo's anticipated cost and an inducement which might make his request more attractive and grantable. By launching the invitation, one of the other-attentive actions, the requester Ming displays his consideration of cost-balancing for revealing that this concern has been Bo "on his mind" and thus showing a degree of altruistic stance.

Taken together, these observations suggest turn designs of requesting are concerned with requestees. In other words, by use of different practices, the requester conveys the brevity or ease of the request, and minimizes the possible cost to the requestee or compensates for the anticipated cost. In doing so, the requester shows a cost-benefit orientation and simultaneously constructs her/himself as being other-attentive.

To sum up, by extending pre-requests, the requester engages in affairs of the requestee and deals with life-worlds of the requestee, conveying her/his concerns for the requestee from the beginning of conversation. In and through pre-requests, the requester assesses the possible cost of the request to the requestee. If the cost to the requestee is higher than what the requester has anticipated, the request will normally be abandoned as in Ex. 5. When the possible cost equals to or is lower than the anticipated cost, the request will be launched as in Ex. 3 and Ex. 8. In terms of turn design of requesting, whatever the practices the requester selects to formulate her/his request turn, they all fully demonstrate the requester's altruistic stance as in pre-requests. These practices are used to design the request as such an action that costs the requestee minimal time, effort or resources. In addition to simplifying the request fulfillment process, a minimal departure from what the requestee is doing or will do is another way to minimize the possible cost to the requestee. Compared with the prior means, the last way focuses on acknowledging the requestee's cost as well as compensating for it, therefore moderating the self-regarding and burdensome nature of the request. Here,

CHAPTER SIX THE DELICACY OF REQUESTING AND SOCIAL SOLIDARITY

what needs to be mentioned is that the altruistic stance is displayed and interactional, it is not a reflection of requesters' psychological state, which is difficult to be estimated and is not the focus of this study.

The practices exploited both in sequence organization and turn design of requesting demonstrate the requester's altruistic orientation when the self-interested nature of requesting cannot be changed. This is the normative way of doing requests. In face-to-face interaction, the situational conditions may play certain roles in fulfilling the altruistic job. For instance, at home, both the wife and the husband are watching TV in sitting room. The wife stands up and heads for the kitchen. Then just at this moment, noticing the wife's orientation, the husband asks the wife to bring him a cup of water from the kitchen. So in this case, it is the physical behavior of the interlocutors that shows the availability of the requestee to do the requested action without causing too much trouble to the requestee. But in telephone conversations, the situational settings of the two parties cannot play any role because the interlocutors do not share the same physical space. As a result, linguistic resources have to be resorted to reduce the possible cost to the requestee when a request is made. With the requestee being taken into consideration, the self-interested nature of requesting can be moderated to some extent. Consequently, the solidary relation between the interlocutors is maintained.

6.3 Social Norms and Social Solidarity

Simply speaking, social norms are the shared ways of behaving in a community. They are taken for granted by the members of the community. The norms would be noticed and recorded only when they are violated, and the party violating the norm would possibly be sanctioned (Enfield & Sidnell, 2019). The social solidarity is achieved and maintained when people behave in the normative way, otherwise the solidary relation might be broken when social norms are neglected.

6.3.1 Requesting sequence and social norms

From observations of the collected data, it is normative to have pre-sequences preceding the requesting turn especially in telephone conversations when the caller and the called cannot see each other. As demonstrated in Chapter Four, the import of pre-requests is to avoid the rejection of the request by means of checking the availability of the requestee or the requested object as well as whether it is convenient for the requestee to do the requested action before it is made. Rejection is a dispreferred action (Schegloff, 2007), the avoidance of which helps the maintenance of the solidary relation between the requester and the requestee.

Ex. 11 [PZD 18/WPF/3:0:00]

```
01          (0.5)
02   东：   喂,h.
03          (0.9)
04   飞：   噢::
05   东：   诶=
06   飞：   =你［说°＞怎么了＜°
07   东：      ［阿飞,.hh 诶::那［个:(.)你借::那个啥啦?=
08   飞：                      ［嗯.
09   东：   =hh.(.)分析天平,
10          (1.1)
11   飞：   对对对在小荀那儿呢.
12          (0.9)
13   东：   啊↑:↓:hhh.在他那呢.
14          (0.7)
15   飞：   对在小荀那儿呢.
```

CHAPTER SIX THE DELICACY OF REQUESTING AND SOCIAL SOLIDARITY

```
16    东：    ↑ang↓hh.也不知道他用完没=
17    飞：    =要-
18            (0.6)
19    飞：    嗯我给他打个电话问一下吧你要用是哇：hh.
20    东：    ((吸气))噢是：hh.现在这：呃：一[个天平他们用=
21    飞：                                  [(  )
22    东：    =着么我：准备测酶呢.
23            (0.9)
24    飞：    行我给他打电话.
25    东：    啊啊.(.)啊.(0.2)好.
26    飞：    他- 他要没用- 没用了就你拿过去啦.
27    东：    啊啊h.
```

In this example, Dong (东) calls Fei (飞) to return the borrowed analytical balance that Fei had lent to Xiao Xun. It is obvious that having established recognition and identification by the voice sample (Lines 02-04), Dong does not produce a request, rather initiates a FPP of a pre-request (Lines 07 & 09) after the inquiry from Fei for the reason for the call (Line 06). In this way, Dong not only passes over the first opportunity to initiate a request, but also checks the availability both of the requester and the requested object. Epistemically speaking (Heritage, 2012), the design of Dong's turn (Lines 07 & 09) which is hearable as confirmation-seeking, shows that Dong knows to some extent Fei is the person who borrowed the analytical balance. On the heels of Fei's confirmation and the provision of more information, Dong seeks the confirmation again (Line 13) and gets what he is seeking (Line 15), which defers his potential request further. After giving the information-receipt token (↑ang↓) (Schegloff, 2007), Dong initiates another FPP of the pre-request (Line 16) to check the availability of the analytical balance, deferring his potential request once more. Note that Fei's latched turn is abandoned (Line 17) and after a gap

(Line 18), it is restarted by self-repair at Line 19 consisting of a promise and a pre-offer. At this moment, Fei's turn design displays that he has identified Dong's prospective action projected by pre-requests. As the sequence progresses, Fei provides a conditional pre-emptive offer (Line 26) after Dong's account for why he needs the analytical balance (Lines 20 & 22).

That Dong passes over three times the opportunity to initiate a request displays his orientation to the social norm here governing the initiation of a request, that is, it is not appropriate to perform a request when the availability of both the requestee and the requested object remains uncertain. And his pre-requests seem to provide ample resources for Fei's pre-emptive offer, which is also a representation of abiding by social norms. The preceding discussion has demonstrated the interactional import of pre-requests in this trajectory as well as the interactional achievement occasioned by them, which is a high maintenance of social solidarity. However, cases where pre-requests do not elicit a pre-emptive offer can also maintain social solidarity, as can be seen in the following example.

Ex. 12 [MA 14/LH/6: 0: 34]

(The following conversation occurs subsequent to a telephone call between Gang and his friend Liu, in which they discuss matters related to their mutual friend's wedding ceremony.)

In this example, Gang requests Liu's player account for an online game. This example clearly demonstrates the requester's awareness of the availability of both the requestee and the requested object in the consideration of not being rejected.

26 刚: [然后: 还有你那个那个那个叫什么, (0.5)
27 呃:: hh. (0.3) 暗黑3的号儿还记不记得了.
28 (0.9)
29 柳: 记得了哇.

CHAPTER SIX THE DELICACY OF REQUESTING AND SOCIAL SOLIDARITY

```
30          (1.1)
31   刚:   你玩儿不玩儿了.
32   柳:   我:-目前不玩儿.
33          (1.2)
34   刚:   好=>你要是不玩儿就行=不过你是不是没密保了<
35          (0.6)
36   柳:   呃::有:了好像.
37          (1.2)
38   刚:   你要是(.)没密保就算啦我我我在网吧:玩儿了.
39          你要说[你:(      )
40   柳:         [有-有了应该.
41          (1.3)
42   刚:   那你找找看然后你给我发微信吧.
43          (0.3)
44   柳:   哦:行了行了行.
```

It is apparently identified that the request is prefaced with the pre-request consisted of three pairs of adjacency pairs (Lines 26-29, 31-32 and 34-36). The first two pairs concern the availability of the requested object. The third pair verifies the security of doing the request, which displays the requester's altruistic consideration as afore-discussed. It can be noted that the subsequent pair of pre-request is made relevant as a next step in the sequence of pre-requests caused by the fruit of the prior. At the very moment, the availability of the requested object is verified and a glimpse of the potential request can be caught. Here Gang (刚) did not initiate his request as if the availability of the requested object were uncertain. This may be due to the SPPs to FPPs of pre-requests being in an unthorough manner and Liu's (柳) withholding of a pre-emptive offer which leaves it to Gang to continue. By providing a pair of contrastive alternatives with the latter overlapped by Liu's response (Lines 38-40), Gang gives evidence that his orientation to the contingency which is being handled around the granting of his request – his request will be produced only if the safe condition of Liu's account is ensured or in other words, he would abort the prospective request for the sake of safety of Liu's account. In this way, Gang displays that the normative sequential import of pre-requests can supply and support a texture in which the unfolding interaction can undergird the initiation of his request, thus maintaining social solidarity.

Furthermore, when pre-requests are blocked, the prospective or potential request will be abandoned, which is a more transparent display of accountability to the social norm that the delivery of a request is contingent on obstacle-free pre-sequences.

Ex. 13 [PZD 18/LAX/9: 0: 00]

The following conversation is between classmates Xun and Dong, one of the key keepers. Xun asks Dong for the key to the laboratory because he is going to do an experiment.

```
01          (0.5)
02   东:    喂,
03   荀:    喂,
04          (0.3)
05   东:    [呃.
06   荀:    [在哪儿呢:
07          (0.5)
08   东:    在外边儿了咋啦h.
09          (1.2)((略有杂音))
10   荀:    外:边儿:
11   东:    呃:
12   荀:    你那个::钥匙在哪儿呢:?
13   东:    [钥匙我拿- 钥匙我拿着呢呀?
14   荀:    [实验室的.
```

CHAPTER SIX THE DELICACY OF REQUESTING AND SOCIAL SOLIDARITY

15		(1.3)
16	荀：	你拿着呢你啥时候回来呀.
17		(0.5)
18	东：	我::hhh.(0.6)明天.
19		(2.1)
20	东：	((笑))
21		(0.5)
22	荀：	明>天啊<,
23	东：	呃::hhh.
24		(0.8)
25	荀：	那行h.吧那就：我们休息吧h.[那就：没办法了.
26	东：	[嗯：

Similar to the previous two examples, Xun (荀) launches the pre-requests in a step-by-step way (Lines 06-18) checking the availability of both the requestee and the requested object and assessing the appropriateness of initiating the potential request. The pre-sequence in this example consists of four question-answer sequences (Lines 06-08, 12-13, 16-18, 22-23), checking the availability of the requestee and the requested object (the key to the lab) respectively. When the requestee is not currently available (Line 18), the request is also aborted instead of asking the requestee come back immediately, which is against the social norm of doing requests.

So it is conspicuous that pre-requests display the requester's orientation to the requestee's capacity and willingness to grant the potential request before the delivery of a request. If no obstacles arise in the pre-sequence, the request will be made following the pre-requests. However, if anything is blocked in the pre-sequence, the request will be abandoned. This is the normative way of doing requests in terms of sequence organization. The following excerpt is another example of abandoning the request.

Ex. 14 ［PZD 18/WH/8：0：00］

(This excerpt is extracted from a telephone call from Wang to his roommate Dong.)

```
01        (0.5)
02   东： 喂,
03        (0.6)
04   汪： 喂,
05        (0.3)
06   汪： 你在实验室没噢你在宿舍没,
07   东： 不在:
08        (0.9)
09   汪： 嗯↑:↓:嗯好吧好吧=
10   东： =怎么啦?h.=
11   汪： =你啥时候- 你啥时候回来(.)晚上吗?
12        (0.4)
13   东： 呃:我(.)回家了.
14        (0.7)
15   汪： 哦↑:↓哦.哦:好吧好吧.
16        (0.4)((杂音))
17   东： 呃::
18        (0.3)
19   汪： 嗯:>嗯嗯<那行那你回吧.啊.
20   东： 呃:[有啥-
21   汪：    [诶(.)诶.
22        (1.1)
23   汪： 没有我我中午我想看一下我电脑里边一张照片了我说
24   东： [噢::
25   汪： [(   )在宿舍呢.ang.
26        (0.2)
```

CHAPTER SIX THE DELICACY OF REQUESTING AND SOCIAL SOLIDARITY

27　东：　噢::[((笑))

In this example, the question-answer sequences in Lines 06-07 and 11-13 serve as pre-sequences for certain action. From the sequence-closing third *okey*, *okey* ("好吧好吧") after each of these question-answer adjacency pairs, it is shown that the answer to the question is not the one anticipated by the questioner which can be evidenced by the question designs (Wu Yaxin & Yang Yongfang, 2019). The turn designs of the two questions show that Wang's (汪) anticipated or preferred answers from Dong (东) are "yes, I'm in the dorm" and "yes, I will come back in the evening" respectively. But Dong's answers are all dispreferred, which blocks the delivery of the projected action. The pursuit made by the answerer Dong (Line 10) shows that he has interpreted the question as a preliminary to some further action instead of a mere information-seeking question. Without receiving a response, Dong re-initiates his pursuit again (Line 20) after the second question-answer sequence (Lines 11-13), at which point Wang produces his request that had been abandoned (Line 23).

It is analyzable that pre-requests, once launched, develop their own interactional dynamic contingency on how responses will be given by the prospective requestee. Wang could have produced the request had Dong's responses been go-aheads at Lines 07 and 13 respectively.

As Bergmann states that: in reporting an event a speaker makes of that event a reportable event. To mention something makes this a mentionable something, that is, a something worth mentioning (Bergmann, 1992: 156), so pre-requests discreetly inquiring display that the event they inquire must be somehow worth inquiring about; and through their very turn designs they conspicuously disclose the information that the requester's reason for inquiring is to assess whether pre-conditions on which the potentially projected request is granted have been met. Pre-requests are a normative part in the requesting sequences, designing to help the requester reduce or avoid the possibility of rejection and the requestee to leak whether there are some difficulties to the grant of the request in advance (Schegloff, 2007). Launching pre-requests, the requester not only maintains the social solidarity, but also displays her/his orientation to the normativity of making requests.

However, it is true that requesting is not always preceded by pre-sequences. When the request is routine between the requester and the requestee, pre-requests are usually unnecessary.

In Example 15, Rong (荣), having achieved recognition and identification (Lines 01-03), directly initiates a request that asks Fei (飞) who is at the library to bring her lunch when going to the canteen (Line 04). In this example, there is a clear display that pre-requests will be omitted when the request is routine between the requester and the requestee.

Ex. 15 [MA 14/YXR/4：0：00]

01　飞：　°喂，秀荣?°
02　荣：　燕飞?
03　飞：　°诶：°
04　荣：　°诶：：你去图- 你去食堂的时候给我带个饭吧?°
05　飞：　噢，行，我一会先回宿舍呀[我还是给你-
06　荣：　　　　　　　　　　　　　[你还-
07　荣：　哦,[好，那回来再说.
08　飞：　　[哦，回去再跟你说哈.

From Fei's lowered voice (Lines 01 & 03), Rong realizes Fei is at the library and subsequently lowers her own voice when making the request in Line 04. This displays that Rong is familiar with Fei's daily routine (namely, she habitually studies at the library and answers the phone quietly). The when-adverbial clause *when you goes to the canteen* ("你去食堂的时候") in the turn design of request is another indication of Rong's knowledge about Fei's daily routine (namely, after studying, she habitually

CHAPTER SIX THE DELICACY OF REQUESTING AND SOCIAL SOLIDARITY

goes to the canteen before coming back to the dormitory). The overlapping talk (Lines 05 & 06) displays that bringing lunch for Rong is what Fei often does on the way back to the dormitory, as they both mention the food for lunch to be brought back simultaneously. Because of the overlapping talk and Fei's delivery that she will return to the dormitory today first, Rong abandons her turn. Then Fei also abandons her turn due to this overlapping talk. Knowing Fei's whereabouts (namely, at the library), Rong can infer that Fei has not been to the canteen yet and can thus help her with the routine request. This explains why the request is directly made without pre-sequences.

This example shows that the absence of pre-requests is neither deviant from the social norm nor harmful to social solidarity. Rather it serves as the clear evidence that straightforward requesting is also social norm-guided action in the situation where fulfilling the request is routine for the requester. Another situation which renders pre-requests unnecessary occurs when request-related issues have been discussed in the previous communications between the requester and the requestee. Furthermore, the pre-sequences would also be hearably redundant when the requestee assumes the requester knows s/he is available to fulfill a low-cost request.

The following call is from Dong, who is an in-service postgraduate studying in another city, to his colleague Li.

Ex 16. [PZD 18/FN/1：0：00]

01   莉：   诶：小东，
02   东：   诶 >白莉< .hh 嗯：：你帮我[问一下[那个- =
03   莉：   [(嗯) [(°咋啦°)
04   东：   =(0.3)嗯：具体是需要些什么材料.
05   (1.2)
06   莉：   .hh 老：天：啊：人家- 人家在通知里面发的了哇没发？
07   (0.3)

08　东：　　.hh（0.4）就是那个:（.）和那个一样吗?

After the identification-recognition sequence, the conversation enters directly into the phase of requesting without pre-requests. The use of the demonstrative word *that*("那个") in the request turn (Line 02) suggests that its referent is mutually identifiable to the requestee. This further demonstrates that request-related matters were previously addressed in their recent communication. Li's (莉) response in Line 06 displays that she fully understands both Dong's referent when using *nage* and the nature of his request. And what her turn launches is a pre-second insert expansion[①] directed to checking the necessity of Dong's request. That is, what Li's turn does is to deal with the type of SPP (namely granting or rejection) to be made to Dong's request by confirmation-seeking in the format of tag question which is delayed by turn-initial inbreath and responses cries (Goffman, 1981) *oh my God* ("老:天:啊:") via elongation. Besides, one more remarkable thing needs to be mentioned is Li's overlapping talk which is in the mid-turn position[②](Line 03). The first onset of Li's overlapping response *en* ("嗯"), though seemingly intrusive, can be heard reasonably as response to Dong's recognition of her. And the second one displays Li's orientation toward the forward movement of Dong's turn by encouraging Dong to present his request.

As it happens, pre-requests are not launched to check whether Li is available and to project what the base action would be (or in other words, to leak some information about the requested action). However, as evidenced by Li's responses (Lines 03 & 06), intersubjectivity between Li and Dong is not at issue, though neither questions about availability nor about projection

---

　　① Pre-second insert expansions which are type-specific as were some of the pre-expansions are preliminary to some particular type of second pair part which has been made relevant next by the type of first pair part to which it is responding (Schegloff, 2007: 106).

　　② When initiated in the mid-turn position, onsets of overlapping talk is a clear display of next speaker's high attentiveness or orientation to the current turn's progressivity including content-adequacy (Drew, 2010; Hayashi, 2012; Jefferson, 1984b).

CHAPTER SIX THE DELICACY OF REQUESTING AND SOCIAL SOLIDARITY

is put forward. And simultaneously from the turn design of the request turn, it can be seen that Dong has ascertained that Li is available or Li is on duty and Li knows what his request exactly is. This is fully accepted by Li. It can be discerned that the reason why there is no pre-requests in Dong's requesting is that the initiation of this request is based on the previous communications between them. Hence, there is no need for launching pre-requests before initiating the request. The same is true in the following example.

Ex. 17 [MA 14/JY/10:0:00]

(Ying had initially called her cousin Zi to borrow a set of high school English textbooks, but did not proceed with borrowing them as the set was incomplete. In the following conversation, Ying calls Zi again to borrow the same set of textbooks.)

```
01    梓：    喂?=
02    英：    =诶小梓?
03            (0.5)
04    梓：    诶,
05    英：    诶[你- 你尽量把你有的你给我拿回来哇=
06    梓：      [嗯,
07    英：    =我刚刚问人家.hh 就是我姑姑家[那个小孩了=
08    梓：                                [嗯,
09    英：    =人家把书人家搬家人家全:给了人啦=一本儿也没
10            丢下.
11            (0.4)
12    梓：    噢行了,[我给你拿回来.
13    英：          [哈.
```

Upon completion of recognition and identification (Lines 01-04) is the introduction of something overtly heard as or readily analyzable as requesting which is Ying's (英) reason for the call (Lines 05, 07 & 09-10). The

· 155 ·

request turn composed of the request proper (Line 05) plus an account (Lines 07 & 09-10), clearly displays that it is designed based on what Zi has known and what she does not know for the time being. That is, instead of using the explicit referent, Ying's request turn is designed to refer to the requested object by *yours or what you have* ("你有的"), which is explicit to both the requester and the requestee, but not to others including us as analysts. And simultaneously it is designed to convey why the request is initiated once more by introducing that there is no other alternatives for her to turn to (e. g. with the extreme case formulation). Similar to Ex. 15 and Ex. 16, Ying's request is fully granted by Zi without possible obstacles which would have been cleared away by pre-requests. The same is the case in the following example.

Ex. 18 [PZD 18/MJ/2: 0: 00]

(This is a phone call from Xu to Dong for he missed Dong's call a moment ago. Xu and Dong are two students under the same supervisor. Xu, who is the junior student, had called Dong, the senior one, to borrow his research proposal for reference. Though his request was granted by Dong, Xu has never received a message from him since then.)

```
01   虚：    诶师兄啊 hh.
02   东：    诶俊虚，
03          (0.3)
04   虚：    啊：就我今天那个((笑))刚- 刚过了做题了没听到
05          ((笑))
06   东：    噢::你去学校[啦？
07   虚：              [(°没°看到)师兄.
08   虚：    啊::我我刚到刚到(.)学校.
09   东：    噢::(0.2)那个：[你告我那个：电话＞呃不是＜那=
10   虚：                 [ang.
11   东：    =个QQ号.
```

CHAPTER SIX THE DELICACY OF REQUESTING AND SOCIAL SOLIDARITY

12   (1.3)
13   虚： QQ 号 hh.
14   东： 对.
15   (0.9)
16   虚： [(怎么啦)
17   东： [你你给我发的微信上吧.
18   (2.1)
19   虚： (那是 hh.)好嗯::噢师兄你说那个:.hh(.)那个开题
20   报告吗? hh.
21   东： 对对对.
22   (1.3)
23   虚： 噢:我给你发微信上啊.
24   东： 嗯.
25   (0.8)
26   虚： 把我的啊 hh.
27   (0.6)
28   东： 不是开题报告你:你给我发到微信上我给你:
29   你不是要那个开题报告嘛.
… (ten lines dealing with problems of intersubjectivity are omitted)
37   虚： 哦:行行行行呢行呢[师兄.
38   东：   [嗯.
39   (0.5)
40   虚： 噢好嘞好嘞[那谢谢师兄哈=
41   东：   [嗯.
42   东： =啊没事没事前段时间比较忙.
43   (0.7)((杂音))
44   虚： 啊::那没[事没事没事啊.

Having got through, Dong's request for Xu's（虚）QQ number（Lines 09 & 11）is placed subsequent to the side sequence（Jefferson, 1972）

· 157 ·

occasioned by Xu's prior account (Lines 06, 08 & "o" at Line 09), which is preceded by the sequence of recognition and identification (Lines 01-02) and the sequence of Xu's account for having missed Dong's call ("o" at Line 06 & Lines 04 & 07). The response is neither granting nor rejection to the request, but an other-initiated repair (Line 13), displaying a problem with hearing or understanding the prior request, especially the requested object. The repair solution is a confirmation which claims that Dong takes the repairable as hearing problem (Line 14) and which is followed by a long gap of (0.9) at Line 15. This gap is analyzably the result of Xu's withholding of talk at the TRP where Dong's turn reaches a possible completion and is calculated as a confusion-displaying device for a further trouble-resolving, namely covertly pursuing a further repair solution from Dong as evidenced by the overlapping talk (Lines 16-17). The aim here is not to give an elaborate analysis of the course of repair, but it can be discerned that the seemingly achieved intersubjectivity (Lines 19-24) turns out to be misunderstanding again (Lines 26-29) and it is not until Line 40 that intersubjectivity is restored and the pending response is made – granting.

The upshot of the analysis so far is threefold. First, Dong's request is actually a delayed granting to Xu's request long time ago, which may be the reason why there is no pre-requests launched. Second, when prior conversation between the interlocuters has involved the current requesting, there is a preference for direct requests over requests companied by pre-requests. That is, pre-requests are omitted more often than not when the issues related to the current request have been talked about in their prior conversation. And without the help of pre-sequences for projecting the prospective base action, the prior conversation is mobilized to handle with misunderstanding in the process. Third, the prior conversation is not always successfully activated at the time when needed. That is, intersubjectivity about the initiated request is not always easily achieved.

CHAPTER SIX THE DELICACY OF REQUESTING AND SOCIAL SOLIDARITY

Sometimes only through great efforts made by both the requester and the requestee can intersubjectivity be established in an intricate way (as is shown in Ex. 18).

The last possibility for the omission of pre-sequences is the requester knows or at least assumes the requestee is available and the request does not cost too much for the requestee.

The following example is a phone call between Feng and Jing who are friends in the same office. Having established connection with Jing (Lines 01-02) and confirmed her recipiency status (Line 04), Feng initiates the request at Lines 05 & 07 directly without pre-requests.

Ex. 19 [LS 15/XF/6:0:00]

01	风:	[喂?
02	晶:	[喂?
03		(0.4)
04	晶:	嗯:
05	风:	晓晶:那个什[么,你帮我看一下就是桌子- 桌子上=
06	晶:	[嗯,
07	风:	=有没有那个钥匙=我怎么好像把(.)钥匙落在办
08		公室人回来了.(1.2)((走动的脚步声))
09	晶:	.hh 钥匙,哪个钥匙呀=

Here again the request is the first action after the opening of this phone call. It demonstrates that the requester Feng (风) knows or assumes the requestee Jing (晶) is still in the office after she left. This assumption may stem from the fact that Feng had returned to her dorm from the office just before the interaction. Jing was working in the office when Feng left, so she was likely still there during this brief interval. Moreover, to check whether keys were left in the office is not a time- and effort-consuming job. Given these factors, it would be redundant to use pre-sequences to check the availability and convenience of the requestee

· 159 ·

before delivering the request.

Based on the aforementioned analysis, it is obvious that these three types of circumstances in which requests are straightforwardly produced have something in common. A first thing is that the canonical telephone opening sequence[①] in mundane conversation is attenuated. A second thing is that in each extract the request, as the requester's reason for call, is produced prior to the anchor position for introducing the first topic. And a third thing is that the way of directly initiating the request conveys that the requester and the requestee have some kind of personally shared access to the initiated request, either by shared knowledge as routine or assumption (as is illustrated in Ex. 15, 19) or by prior communications (as is illustrated in Ex. 16, 17, 18). It is also obvious that these circumstances sometimes intersect with one another. Here, one phenomenon cannot be neglected is that people will call for help directly in an emergency (especially a life-threatening emergency). Although it is not collected in the present data, it actually belongs to one kind of common sense knowledge, and thereby it requires no further exemplification. These findings illustrate how social norms are oriented to in requesting sequence, especially in pre-requests and how social solidarity is maintained in pre-requests driven by social norms. They also demonstrate that pre-requests are made explicit an interactional norm in the requesting sequence. This does not mean that the norm-governed orientations to pre-requests must always be explicitly exhibited. In fact, deviations from the norm which are seemingly norm-violating and solidarity-threatening serve as powerful evidence for displaying pre-requests as a social norm.

---

① According to Schegloff, the canonical telephone opening sequence is composed of four pairs of adjacency pairs, (namely, summons-answer, identification-recognition, greetings exchange and exchange of "how are you?"s responses), after which the first topic (namely, the reason for call) is introduced in the anchor position (Schegloff, 1986).

CHAPTER SIX THE DELICACY OF REQUESTING AND SOCIAL SOLIDARITY

6.3.2 Turn designs of requesting and social norms

Normally the requesting turn is designed by three lexical-syntactic formats – the imperative, the interrogative and the declarative in Mandarin Chinese. The choice of one format while the other two alternatives are available is systematically related to the requester's assessment of her/his entitlement to request something from others or to request others to do something and the contingency possibly involved in the granting of the request (Curl & Drew, 2008), which is clear evidence for exhibiting the requester's normative orientation toward the underlying social norm.

6.3.2.1 The choice of imperatives, interrogatives and declaratives

A. Imperatives

Imperatives are a practice deployed by the requester to claim high entitlement to having her/his request granted and to show awareness of low contingency surrounding the granting of her/his request. For instance, in the previously discussed Example 12 (numbered as Ex. 12′), Gang asks for Liu's player account for an online game. This example is a highly clear demonstration of the requester's entitlement to request what is being requested and his awareness of the associated contingency about the granting of his request.

Ex. 12′[MA 14/LH/6:0:34]

26　刚：　　　　　[然后:还有你那个那个那个叫什么, (0.5)
27　　　　呃::hh. (0.3) 暗黑3的号儿还记不记得了.
28　　　　(0.9)
29　柳：　记得了哇.
30　　　　(1.1)
31　刚：　你玩儿不玩儿了.
32　柳：　我:-目前不玩.

33		(1.2)
34	刚：	好=>你要是不玩儿就行=不过你是不是没密保了<
35		(0.6)
36	柳：	呃::<u>有</u>:了好像.
37		(1.2)
38	刚：	你要是(.)没密保就算啦我我我在网吧:玩儿了.
39		你要说[你:-
40	柳：	[有- 有了应该.
41		(1.3)
42	刚：	那你找找看然后你给我发微信吧.
43		(0.3)
44	柳：	哦:行了行了行.

Before making his request, Gang displays his awareness of the availability of both the requestee and the requested object (Lines 26-29, 31-32 and 34-36). By providing alternatives, Gang displays his awareness of possible and potential impediment to the granting of the request, which is possibly due to several gaps and the turn-constructional practices employed in Liu's answers to pre-requests displaying his hesitancy and uncertainty (Lines 29, 36). Finding himself talking in overlap with Liu's response (Lines 39-40), Gang drops out as is shown by his cutting-off and confirms the abscence of any potentially relevant contingency. Right at this point of his checking being confirmed, and following a gap at Line 41 possibly due to the prior overlapping talk, Gang initiates the request in the imperative format prefaced by na ("那"). In terms of this turn design, Gang claims high entitlement and low contingency: because the contingency which is explored in and through pre-requests potentially surrounding the granting of his request is eliminated and thereby Gang has good reason for considering his request reasonable and easily to be granted. The following example also displays that the requester orients to entitlement and contingency when initiating a

CHAPTER SIX THE DELICACY OF REQUESTING AND SOCIAL SOLIDARITY

request.

Ex. 20 [PZD 18/LAX/8:0:00]

(This telephone conversation occurs between classmates Xiong and Dong. Xiong is a probationary Party member and Dong is responsible for his training.)

```
01   雄：   .h(0.4)喂，
02   东：   ↓喂.
03          (0.8)
04   雄：   你在哪呢::¿
05          (0.9)
06   东：   实验室:hh.=
07          (0.8)
08   雄：   实验室啊你给我写个东西呗.
09   东：   修:¿个东西¿
10          (0.6)
11   雄：   .h写个东西写:写:写:[个东西.
12   东：                    [(那-)
13   东：   写啥呢.
14          (1.0)
15   雄：   写那个党员什么::呃:(0.3)就是::
16          ((翻纸的声音))(0.3)培养联系人嘛什么的.
17   东：   ang:那你拿过来哇hh.
```

In this example, Xiong (雄) initiates his request in the format of an imperative (Line 08). By such an imperative format, Xiong displays no orientation toward the requestee Dong's (东) abilty or willingness to grant, thereby displaying that his request is considered not dependent on any other contingencies except his current whereabouts which has been ascertained by the pre-request at Lines 04-06. Simultaneously, by such an imperative format, Xiong claims his entitlement to make the request, which might be associated with or mobilized by Dong's obligation. And the final particle *bei* ("呗") displays the ease with which his request can be fulfilled or granted. In other words, the use of *bei* displays that Xiong treats no other contingencies as relevant to Dong's ability to grant his request (i.e., there is no problem granting his request) and simultaneously indexes the ease with which Dong can fulfill the requested action.

B. Interrogatives

In contrast to imperatives for conveying the requester's assessment of one's high entitlement and low contingency to produce a request, interrogatives including tag questions and disjunctive questions (Li & Thompson, 1989) can be used to downgrade one's entitlement and simultaneously to upgrade contingency to initiate a request.

Ex. 21 clearly illustrates the employment of a tag question to downgrade the requester's entitlement and to upgrade the associated contingency when a request is implemented.

Ex. 21 [MA 14/TY/7:0:00]

(This conversation is called from Hui at the dormitory to her roommate Yu who is studying at the library.)

```
01    惠：    喂？hhh.
02    雨：    °怎么 [了-°
03    惠：         [喂，小雨？=
04    雨：    =哎=
05    惠：    =你在图书馆了:?=
06    雨：    =嗯:在了，
07            (0.4)
08    惠：    咱们去吃饭吧？((笑))=
09    雨：    =你饿啦？
10            (0.5)
11    惠：    嗯:没- 我没有饿，但是我瞌睡的不行((笑))
```

CHAPTER SIX   THE DELICACY OF REQUESTING AND SOCIAL SOLIDARITY

```
12   雨:   行嘞,.hhh 那我那个:.hhh 那我就在那个, (0.4) 呃:
13        餐厅门口等着你.((杂音))
14        (1.1)
15   惠:   嗯::行呢,
16   雨:   嗯:,.hhh 那个.hhh 你帮我带上餐具吧=装在一块儿
17        你帮我提着,行吧?
18   惠:   嗯:行呢.
```

At Lines 16-17, subsequent to her elongated *en* ("嗯:"), the sequence-closing thirds (Schegloff, 2007: 118) functioning to end the prior sequence, Yu formats her request as a tag question. By attaching a tag question *Please take it for me with yours together to the canteen, Okey?* ("装在一块儿你帮我提着行吧?") to the imperative *Please take my tableware for me.* ("你帮我带上餐具吧"), the high entitlement to produce her request and the low contingency in granting her request carried by the imperative are lowered and upgraded respectively. That is, it is clear that the imperative sentence not only specifies how to implement the initiated request and acknowledges Hui's cost to do the request, but also suggests that Hui also has the habit of taking tableware to the canteen, by which Yu claims her high entitlement to initiating her request – she is not asking for a special trip for taking her tableware for Hui is going to the canteen (which is clearly presented in prior sequences). And simultaneously by the imperative sentence, Yu considers *taking the tableware together to the canteen* being the only relevant contingency for granting her request: because (1) they are going to the canteen and meeting at the entrance of the canteen, and (2) when these two agreements are reached, Yu and Hui are at the library and dormitory respectively, granting her request is normally unproblematic. Nonetheless, the question tag in the rising tone, compared with the final particle *ba* ("吧") in imperatives, grammatically explicitly invites Hui to make a response – yes or no. In terms of the constraint that FPPs impose upon SPPs (Sacks, Schegloff & Jefferson, 1974), the tag question here functions to mark the current turn as a question to be answered (or especially seeking confirmation) instead of directive-implicative utterance to be consented to or not. In doing so, Yu displays her awareness of possible rejection to be made by Hui due to some possible contingencies that she did not anticipate, thereby upgrading the contingency and accordingly downgrading the entitlement to certain degree as well.

It is worth noting that the request turn is composed of multi-TCUs: an imperative which is appropriate for the pariticualr sequential position to initiate a request is latched by a tag question (Line 16). It is in such a way that (1) the request turn is expanded, turning out as a tag question; (2) a dynamic process is exhibited in which both the entitlement and contingency are adjusted and (3) the dynamics of entitlement and contingency in the unfolding interaction is revealed. This retroactively suggests that entitlement and contingency are not settled in the course of the request initiation and degrees of entitlement and contingency are displayed or claimed through the way in which the requester formats her/his request turn.

Another practice for displaying lower entitlement and higher contingency than those displayed by imperatives involves the employment of disjunctive questions. The following example is a case in point.

Ex. 22 [PZD 18/WH/1:0:00]

(This is a conversation between roommates. Han who is doing experiment at the laboratory calls Dong resting at the dormitory to fetch his package.)

```
01   东：    .tch 喂，
02           (0.8)
03   涵：    啊喂东哥，
04   东：    呃：
05   涵：    呃- 你你那个闲着没.
06   东：    ((杂音))噢:((杂音))
```

CHAPTER SIX THE DELICACY OF REQUESTING AND SOCIAL SOLIDARITY

```
07          (0.5)
08   涵：   你(.)能不能帮我取个快递呀.
09   东：   呃在哪儿呢,hhh.
10   涵：   就唯品会的：呃：人家就四四点半就走了我说
11          .h(.)我[我也过不去：
12   东：        [好.
13   东：   嗯嗯：=
```

Han's employment of a disjunctive question (*A-not-A questions*) displays relative low entitlement and high contingency in making his request through at least three features of the turn design: (1) in the syntactic format of an interrogative, it requires an answer both grammatically and normatively (Schegloff, 1972); (2) the disjunctive question displays his lack of certainty about his entitlement to the request and acknowledges that there might be some other contingencies for granting his request. That is, this format shows Han's presumption of a possible rejection to be forthcoming, and thereby the entitlement is low and contingency is high. And (3) the *A-not-A questions* do not project any preference for its response in terms of turn design. That is, compared with the tag question which is grammatically designed to display a preference[①] for a "yes" answer used in the prior example, this *A-not-A question* does not show a preference for a "yes" or "no" answer. Thus, Han's design indexes lower entitlement and higher contingency compared with those displayed by tag questions.

In terms of sequential position, the relative high contingency is alluded to in the pre-requests in which a hedging response is provided (Line 06), Han does not further check Dong's immediate availability and thus, at this moment there might be some contingencies that possibly prevent his request

---

[①] Polar questions typically display the speakers' preference for one of them over the other (Hayano, 2013: 405).

from being granted, for instance, Dong would have done experiment. That is, at this point to initiate a request might be rejected due to unanticipated contingencies. But after half second gap a request is produced in the *A-not-A question* format which clearly displays Han's awareness of this condition and leaves room for Dong to reject. Besides, it can be noticed that subsequent to the request an inquiry about the information necessary to fulfill the initiated request (namely, where to fetch the package) gets more information than what is inquired. As it happens, Han's response, incongruent with a conversational economy of information (Levinson, 2012), not only identifies the name of the express but also provides an account for why this request is initiated. This account here serves to present the urgency of the initiated request and present his inability to get the package back on time as well. In doing so, Han displays the evidence of his entitlement to initiate this request, that is, his request is somewhat reasonable, therefore expecting his request to be granted.

In Ex. 21 and 22, requesters use different lexical-syntactic formats exhibiting their relative lower entitlement and higher contingency to deliver a request. In other cases, however, requesters show even lower entitlement and higher contingency when producing a request through *I want/say*-declaratives as illustrated in the following examples.

C. Declaratives

The deployment of *I want/say*-declaratives as compared to interrogatives demonstrates the requester's orientation both to her/his request being problematic and to known or possibly anticipated contingencies connected to the request, namely low entitlement and high contingency. The two examples below clearly illustrate the *I want/say* -declaratives as a practice of claiming low entitlement and high contingency to produce a request respective.

Ex. 23 [PZD 18/WAM/2: 0: 00]

(Ai calls Dong, her classmate, to borrow the crucible. Dong's laboratory

CHAPTER SIX　THE DELICACY OF REQUESTING AND SOCIAL SOLIDARITY

is next to hers.)

```
01   艾:     呃- 东哥,
02   东:     喂.
03          (0.6)
04   艾:     诶. 你- 你不在实验室吗?=你们实验室开着门呢:?
05          (0.2)
06   东:     啊:我不在 h.
07          (0.3)
08   东:     怎么了?=
09   艾:     =哦:
10          (.)
11   艾:     >你们实验室谁在实验室呢开着门呢<
12          >我想用一下<你们的那个(.).h 坩埚:
13          (0.4)
14   东:     坩埚:?
15          (0.4)
16   艾:     嗯:
17          (1.3)
18   东:     嗯:::hh.(0.2)下午吧:下午我过去.
```

Here Lines 04-06 is a pre-sequence in which Ai (艾) asks Dong's (东) whereabouts. From this pre-sequence, Ai gets to know that Dong is currently not available to fulfill her request, namely, lending his crucible to her. This clearly increases the contingency of granting the request. Although the door of Dong's lab is open, it would not be appropriate for Dong to allow Ai to get the crucible by herself because the lab is shared with other classmates. Knowing this as common sense between the interlocutors, Ai has low entitlement to deliver her request in the syntactic formats of imperatives or interrogatives. The declarative "I want to use your crucible" displays the requester's low entitlement to issue the request and the high contingency of

· 169 ·

granting the request by the requestee.

In the following example, Jing（静）, the requester, formulates her request in the *I say*-declarative with slight variances.

Ex. 24 [DIG 16/ZJ/1：0：00]

01　淑：　喂:?咋了，美女，
02　　　　(0.9)
03　静：　喂:?
04　淑：　诶，
05　　　　(1.0)
06　静：　你在不在学校了:
07　淑：　我在呢呀？怎么啦？
08　静：　嗯:上自习还是干嘛了.
09　淑：　我准备吃饭了这会儿hhh.
10　　　　(1.2)
11　静：　准备吃饭了:=
12　淑：　=嗯，你有事儿呢:？=
13　静：　=在文瀛？
14　淑：　我［还没过去呢，
15　静：　　［(还是-)
16　静：　还是令德了.
17　淑：　还没［过去hhh.-
18　静：　　　［嗯，我- 我拿的- 我拿好多东西我回不去了，
19　　　　我说让你过来，(.)我放你-((笑))放你后面，((笑))
20　淑：　噢:［行，行行行，你在哪儿呢？

Similar to the above example, there is a long pre-sequence (Lines 06-17) before the request turn (Line 19). From the pre-sequence the caller Jing accesses the information about the availability of Shu and the cost of her request to Shu. In addition, pre-requests in this example fully demonstrate the requester's orientation toward the contingency involved in granting her

170

CHAPTER SIX   THE DELICACY OF REQUESTING AND SOCIAL SOLIDARITY

request. Passing over at least three opportunities (Lines 03, 08 & 13) to introduce a request, Jing explores the possibility of her request to be granted in a progressive manner. By pre-requests, Jing ascertains that Shu is at school now (Lines 06-07) and is not occupied (Lines 08-09), but she does not identify whether it is convenient for Shu to grant her request, namely Shu is undecided about where to go for dinner (Lines 13-17). In such a case, though, there is one contingency that might prevent her request from being granted: if Shu will go to *Lingde*, the one far from the school gate. Thus by using the *I say*-declarative format, Jing displays her awareness of the low entitlement to initiate the request and the high contingency of granting her request.

The *I say*-declarative that Jing chooses constructs her as someone who is merely doing a reported speech. According to Voloshinov (1971: 149), reported speech is speech within speech, message within message, and at the same time also speech about speech, message about message. That is, reported speech is simultaneously a report of a previous thought or locution and part of a new sequence used for a different purpose (Holt, 2000: 433). This is clearly evident in Jing's *I say*-declarative. In doing so, Jing does dual action simultaneously: she not only makes a report of her original or previous thought but also conveys or reproduces the action – request which the reported speech was designed to implement. Shu's response at Line 20 shows that she has heard what Jing says and what she is doing by saying of it. Jing's format of her request proper avoids making a claim to know that Shu can or will pick her up, assumptions that would be embodied by, say, imperatives or interrogatives, thus leaving it up to Shu's decision or judgment and setting loose constraint on Shu's response like Ai in Ex. 23. In this way, Jing shows her assessment of the low entitlement as well as the high contingency associated with her request.

Note that the request is placed subsequent to an account (Line 18) which overlaps with the preceding turn (Line 17) in progress. By providing an account for her request, Jing foregrounds her inability, marking the upcoming request somewhat reasonable. The precise onset of Jing's account shows that she is highly monitoring Shu's ongoing talk for places where it is relevant to make a response. Her account begins when Shu's turn is adequately recognized[①] as an answer for her inquiry: her forthcoming request has contingency that she does not anticipate. Although the contingency is high, it is not settled. That is, there is a possibility that the contingency could be satisfied before Jing's request to be granted, because the choice of the canteen for dinner has not been made yet. Note also that the sequential environment where this request is initiated has something in common with that in Ex. 23: pre-requests does not clear up the obstacles to granting the upcoming request. However, it is slightly different from the previous one: it is possible that the obstacle can be removed in this example, whereas it is impossible that the obstacle is cleared up in Ex. 23.

6.3.2.2 The relationship between different choices of lexical-syntactic formats and entitlement & contingency

As the foregoing analysis of the requester's employment of lexical-syntactic formats for initiating a request demonstrates, the choice of one lexical-syntactic format instead of other alternatives is highly related to the requester's assessment of her/his entitlement to initiate the request and the contingency associated with granting the request (Curl & Drew, 2008). Both the entitlement and the contingency are something that is negotiated between the requester and the requestee in the request sequence, especially the pre-requests. What is important and relevant to the requester is whether, and to what extent, s/he through her/his interaction with the requestee shows

---

① Here, as Jefferson's study (1983) that it is the adequacy rather than the completeness of a prior turn that is oriented to by recipients, the account displays Jing's orientation to the potential contingency and her urgent need for changing the current situation into a more positive one.

CHAPTER SIX   THE DELICACY OF REQUESTING AND SOCIAL SOLIDARITY

that s/he is entitled to initiate the request and the contingency surrounding the granting of the request can be satisfied before the request can be granted. Entitlement and contingency, then, are not settled and predefined, but instead are negotiated, conveyed and accomplished through the way in which both the requester and the requestee format their contributions and ultimately expressed and embodied in the format by which the requester initiates her/his request (personal discussion with Prof. Wu). To be specific, the entitlement is, in everyday interactions among friends and family, often grounded in the local trajectory of ongoing action (Zinken, 2015: 24). It emerges bit by bit from the unfolding request sequence and is changing dynamically as the progressing sequence. In other words, it can be understood as sequentially invoked, which can be dynamically assessed in the train of current turns or TCUs (personal discussion with Prof. Wu). Judging the degree of the entitlement of a request is assessed on the grounds of requestability, while that of the contingency needs to make reference to the grantability of a request. Grantability can be locally evidenced by the existence or not and the smoothness of the pre-sequences. When normally there are pre-sequences and none of it is blocked, the contingency of a request is low, otherwise, when there is no pre-sequences or the pre-sequences are blocked, the contingency will grow. The high grantability indicates the low contingency of a request and vice versa. Requestability mainly depends on whether the request is reasonable, or in other words, it is more requestable if the degree of difficulty for the requester to fulfill the requested action is higher than that to be fulfilled by the requestee. The easier for the requestee to fulfill and the harder for the requester to fulfill, then the higher the requestability is, otherwise, the harder for the requestee to fulfill and the easier for the requester to fulfill, then the lower the requestability is. The requestability is contingently balancing the entitlement of a speaker making a request. When the requetability is high, the entitlement of the requester is high, while the entitlement will be low if the requestability is low (ideas inspired from Prof. Wu).

Through imperatives, the requester displays the orientation that s/he is highly entitled to initiate the request and considers her/his request as noncontingent. That is, the grounds for making the request is reasonable given the sequential environment and there are no other conditions for granting the request. In contrasting, by formatting a request as declaratives, the requester shows the stance that the request is delivered on the basis of low entitlement and high contingency. That is, the requester does not have or cannot show good reason for considering her/his request reasonable given the current circumstances and there are certain conditions that cannot be satisfied for granting the request. In addition, there is one in-between case: by producing a request employing interrogatives (including tag questions and disjunctive questions), the requester claims that s/he is to some extent entitled to make the request and granting the request is subject to some uncertain contingencies. That is, the reasonableness of the requester as grounds for initiating the request is acknowledged but it is not so solid, and there are some possibly potential conditions that might not be satisfied for granting the request.

As displayed in above examples, these three lexical-syntactic formats are constructed along a continuum: from the high entitlement and low contingency demonstrated by the deployment of imperatives, to the relative high entitlement and relative low contingency displayed by the choice of interrogatives and finally to the low entitlement and high contingency showed by the employment of declaratives. In other words, there is a progressive decrease in entitlement displayed by imperatives, interrogatives and declaratives, whereas there is a progressive increase in contingency showed by these three formats. Figure below presents the entitlement and contingency continuum. This pattern is very similar to the relevant findings made in English conversations (Curl & Drew 2008).

CHAPTER SIX THE DELICACY OF REQUESTING AND SOCIAL SOLIDARITY

The analysis of examples in this subsection is an explicit show that the robustness of the requester's orientation to the normative organization of initiating a request and in the meantime the specific ways in which these normative practices of pre-requests, goings-in-front-of requests and turn design of requests are adapted to local interactional circumstances.

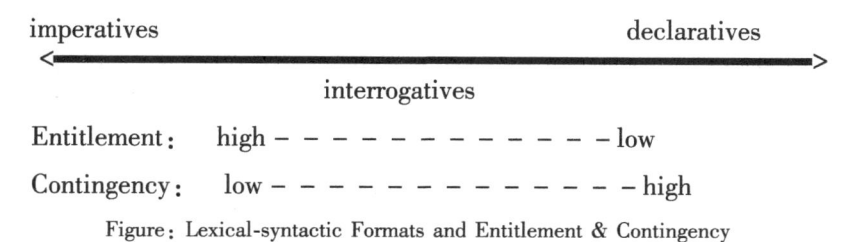

```
   imperatives                                declaratives
   <─────────────────────────────────────────────>
                    interrogatives
   Entitlement:  high – – – – – – – – – – – low
   Contingency:  low  – – – – – – – – – – – high
```
                Figure: Lexical-syntactic Formats and Entitlement & Contingency

The relation between entitlement/contingency and the syntactic formats of requesting displays the specific social norms constraining the choice of syntactic format in doing requesting. When a requester has high entitlement and the request has low contingency, imperatives are the frequently used syntactic format when the request is made. Conversely, if a requester has low entitlement and the request has high contingency, *I want/say* declaratives are usually resorted to when the request is made. People choose the proper syntactic format to make a request in congruence with their entitlement and the contingency of the request, in other words, people usually follow the social norms in requesting. Otherwise, they would be morally sanctioned. When people behave in the normative way, social solidarity will be achieved and maintained. If the social norm is violated, the solidary relation between the interlocutors will also be harmed.

6.4 Delicacy, Altruism, Social Norms and Social Solidarity

In this section the relationship between delicacy, altruism, social norms and social solidarity will be considered.

6.4.1 Altruism: the intrinsic engine for delicacy

It seems to be an paradox: when initiating a request, the requester would show concerns for the requestee's interest or do other-attentiveness, due to the property or nature of requesting as mentioned in Chapter 1. Despite this doubt, evidences for the requester's doing other-attentiveness are scattered in the above discussed examples.

The first self-evident feature of delicacy in requesting is delay, namely, deferring the initiation of a request either by pre-requests or goings-in-front-of requests. Both pre-requests and goings-in-front-of requests are designed to be recognizable to the requestee as foreshadowing what is forthcoming is a request, which can be blocked by the requestee's response. For instance, a prospective request is aborted in Ex. 5. "Are you in the office now?" gets a blocked response "I'm at the dorm.", suggesting the prospective requester that a request will be rejected and providing the requester a resource for avoiding a dispreferred response, therefore maintaining the social solidarity. Other-attentiveness is manifested in the requester's abortion of her request, for the requester recognized that the extra cost must be added to the requestee if this request were initiated after the pre-request. Besides, thanks to the high projectability of pre-requests, the prospective requestee is provided an opportunity for offering. If pre-requests successfully solicit help from the prospective requestee, then the trajectory of conversation will be changed, avoiding initiation of a request and creating the prospective requestee as an image of a helpful offerer, thereby maintaining social solidarity. In terms of the pre-pre, other-attentiveness or altruistic action is manifested mainly in two phases: (1) the pre-pre provides an opportunity for the requestee to reject the projected request theoretically, and (2) in the phase of preliminary

CHAPTER SIX THE DELICACY OF REQUESTING AND SOCIAL SOLIDARITY

(including pre-mentions or pre-conditions, or both), by offering more information relevant to the projected request, the requester provides another opportunity for the requestee to reject the projected request theoretically on the one hand, s/he also checks whether there are obstacles to the requestee's granting on the other. For the possibility of the requestee's failure to recognizing the offered information cannot be excluded, in such a situation, a request is normally aborted to avoid a dispreferred response and simultaneously to avoid additional cost caused to the requestee. By contrast, goings-in-front-of requests do not check availability as pre-requests do, instead goings-in-front-of requests by troubles-telling or bridging cushion the initiation of a request and avoid the abruptness of delivering a request, indexing unassuredness of possible cost of the prospective request to the requestee.

The second feature of delicacy in requesting is minimization often displayed in turn designs, which is achieved through minimal portrayal of the cost or imposition of the request, minimization of the possible cost to or imposition on the requestee and balance of the cost to the requestee by providing benefits as appreciations. Other-attentive or altruistic laminations are exquisitely displayed by these three ways. The first one conveys the brevity or ease of the request, constructing the request as such an action that costs the requestee minimal time, effort or resources. The second way mainly resorts to requestee's minimal diversion from what s/he is doing or will do so as to minimize the possible cost to the requestee. And the last way directly compensates for the requestee's future cost. All these three ways contribute to moderating the self-interested and burdensome nature of a request, thereby showing other-attentiveness.

The third feature of delicacy in requesting is also displayed in turn designs: the very choices of lexical-syntactic formats. As is shown in the data, a request for objects or actions is normally implemented through one of three lexical-syntactical formats: imperatives, interrogatives and declaratives.

Given the sequential position a request is initiated, the choice of one instead of the other two alternatives not only displays the requester's orientation to her/his entitlement to requesting and contingency possibly associated with request's granting, which is a manifestation of delicacy in turn designs, but also shows the requester's altruistic stance. This altruistic stance is indexed by the imposition of the request on the requestee. The degree of the imposition of a request on the requestee displayed by imperatives, interrogatives and declaratives is decreasing and the degree of showing concerns for the requestee is increasing.

It is not difficult to discern that delicacy in requesting offers an indexical relationship to the altruistic stance or other-attentiveness portrayed both in requesting sequence and in turn designs of requesting. That is, delicacy displayed in requesting demonstrates the workings of intrinsic engine – altruism.

6.4.2 Social norms: the realization of delicacy

Social norms are both the consequence and facilitator of social interactions (personal discussion with Prof. Wu). Just as people are oriented to social norms in social interactions, so initiating a request (as it happens) is social norms-oriented.

The above examples, minutely sketched, are supposed to suffice to demonstrate how delicacy displayed in requesting is realized by linguistic and non-linguistic resources on the grounds of social norms. Social norms in requesting are mainly generalized from two respects: requesting sequences and turn designs of requesting. To begin with, it is identified that pre-requests, a component of most requesting sequences, are of crucial importance in forwarding the sequence to the FPP of the projected action at hand – a request and also provide an illustration of the role of timing played in sequence organization as well. As is shown in these examples, normally

CHAPTER SIX THE DELICACY OF REQUESTING AND SOCIAL SOLIDARITY

when pre-requests are payed off by a pre-emptive offer, the initiation of projected request will be avoided. When the FPP of pre-requests gets go-ahead responses, the request will be initiated. And when the FPP of pre-requests gets blocked responses, the request normally will be abandoned. In requesting sequences, pre-requests are designed for checking availability of the requestee or the requested object, and overwhelmingly successfully so. For instance, in Ex. 4, pre-requests are hearable as something asked not in its own right, instead, as a harbinger of or preliminary to something contingently to follow, depending on the requestee's response. That is why a question as FPP of pre-requests like *Are you at school* often gets a returned question like *What's up* ("咋了"). The "What's up" asker, namely the requestee knows that s/he is not being asked for whether s/he is at school, but s/he is being asked about her/his availability. Similarly, the pre-pre is often met with go-ahead response. And goings-in-front-of requests by troubles-telling or bridging often get moved forward smoothly and make a request initiated (or sometimes successfully solicit offer).

That a request can be recognizable as a request is a matter of position and composition: where the talk is produced and how it is constructed (Clift, Drew & Local, 2013). For instance, in Ex. 3, displayed delicacy is transparent from the outset, illustrating the requester's normative orientation to initiating a request through the specific way in certain sequential position. That is, the requester, unassured of the availability of the requestee, passes over three opportunities to initiate her request. The declarative used to implement her request reflects the requester's assessment of her low entitlement to launch the request and high contingency involved in granting the request. And at the same time, the requestee also displays a clear orientation toward the social norm that organizes or governs the initiation of a request. That request can be recognized as a request is through the same practice by which the requester delivers the request and is under the regiment of the same social norm to which the request is oriented when initiating the request. It shows the reflexive nature of social norms.

There is a reflexive relationship between delicacy built in requesting and social norms of initiating a request. That is, what pre-requests are deployed to do is explained by the pre-requests launched before the initiation of a request. The requester knows that imperatives used to implement a request display high entitlement and low contingency and s/he assumes that the requestee also knows it by the right choice of the imperative in interaction. The displayed delicacy in requesting suggests the requester's orientation to the social norm of initiating a request, while that the requester abide by the social norm of initiating a request constructs delicacy in the process of initiating a request.

6.4.3 Social solidarity: the aim of being delicate

Pre-sequences are used to avoid the dispreferred response to the base sequence, thereby increasing the likelihood of the base sequence having a solidary outcome (Clayman, 2002; Heritage, 1984a; Schegloff, 2007). Besides, pre-sequences can possibly cause a new interactional trajectory which can enhance solidarity (Clayman, 2002), that is a pre-emptive sequence is initiated.

Pre-requests with two interactional functions are overwhelmingly used in request sequences. When pre-requests successfully solicit offer from the prospective requestee, the preference for offers over requests (Sacks, 1992; Schegloff, 2007) are realized and solidarity is enhanced. That is, in terms of sequence organization, the pre-emptive offer leads to a compact trajectory of interaction. In terms of imposition, the prospective requester adds no imposition on the prospective requestee due to the absence of the prospective request. Conversely, the request to be initiated is changed into an offer, which should and could be met with a preferred response, namely the acceptance of the offer.

Any time one is engaged in social interaction, one's actions are of real consequence to the social relationship currently being exercised (Enfield, 2006: 412). Just as each little choice we make in communicative interaction can be assessed for its optimality for information exchange, it can equally be assessed for its optimality for maintaining (or forging) the current social relationship at an appropriate level of intensity or intimacy (ibid.). The choice of different lexical-syntactic formats displays how the requester delicately and exquisitely maintains social solidarity or solidary social relationships when initiating a request which somewhat harms the interest of the requestee. Therefore, social solidarity is the outcome of obeying social norms which are the realization of delicacy.

6.5 Summary

This chapter provides an interpretation of delicacy in requesting in terms of social solidarity, social norms and altruism. They are deeply interlocked.

Social actions are social norms-grounded. The social solidarity is achieved and maintained when people behave in the normative way. As demonstrated in the above extracts, when initiating a request, as social actors, the requester is regimented by social norms which involves the above-mentioned practices and are taken for granted. The requester exploits these practices as resources for launching a request as the way it is. That is, while in initiating a request, the requester is doing being delicate or doing delicacy. In this respect, it directly demonstrates that the reflexive relationship between the deployed practices and delicacy. In mean time, doing delicacy or doing being delicate in requesting can be interpreted as evidence that altruism is the underlying engine for doing delicacy. That is, doing delicacy in requesting can be analyzable as evidence in favor of the requestee and showing considerateness to the requestee rather than the requester her/himself. In this respect, doing delicacy is manifestation of altruism and altruism is the incentive of doing delicacy, namely they are in an indexical relation.

To sum up, doing delicacy can be realized by social norms-abiding by. Doing delicacy can show the requester's altruistic stance, which could achieve and maintain social solidarity or a harmonious relationship. And social solidarity is the achievement of doing delicacy while requesting.

CHAPTER SEVEN   CONCLUSION

In this chapter, findings and contributions of the present study will be summarized, implications will be discussed and limitations and suggestions for further study will also be pointed out.

7.1   Findings and Contributions of the Present Study

Adopting the methodology of Conversation Analysis, the present study explores delicacy in requesting in telephone conversations. As Schegloff states, the aim of conversation analysis is to find and explicate organizations of practice that underwrite all interaction (2010: 40). The present study, based on everyday conversations, has unraveled the practices by which delicacy is constructed in requesting and by which requesting is delivered. It also has interpreted delicacy in requesting from the perspective of social solidarity, social norms and altruism. The major findings of the present study are summarized as:

The study demonstrates that in terms of the maneuver of sequence organization, delicacy in requesting is constructed by pre-sequences including pre-requests and goings-in-front-of-requests. Pre-requests are used to address three matters: (1) to test the waters (Clayman, 2002: 239), that is, to check preconditions or possibilities of the upcoming request being granted; (2) to postpone the initiation of a request sequentially and (3) to solicit a pre-emptive offer without explicitly launching a request. The pre-pre as a different kind of type-specific pre-requests usually creates the space for introduction of background, pre-condition or both, which enables the sequence to proceed to the initiation of a request and delays the request sequentially. Different from pre-requests, pre-pres project a forthcoming request by metalanguage and create a slot to provide preconditions or background information related to the request, which reduce the possibility of getting rejection from the requestee to the upcoming request.

The second part begins with an illustration of delicacy in goings-in-front-of-requests, which is categorized into two types: generic goings-in-front-of-requests and type-specific goings-in-front-of-requests. It shows that generic goings-in-front-of-requests, prior to the request sequence, is employed to show the requester's concern for the requestee, creating a friendly conversation atmosphere and cushioning the initiation of a request. Type-specific goings-in-front-of-requests is normally a troubles-telling sequence, which serves to defer the initiation of a request as well as to legitimize the initiation of a request, especially when the trouble has not been solved. Besides, it also has a potential function to solicit help from the prospective requester as an alternative to a request. Bridging is another kind of type-specific goings-in-front-of-requests, which does favorable social actions to the requestee, paving the way for initiating a request. All the work done by the requester resorting to pre-requests or goings-in-front-of-requests demonstrates that requesting is treated delicately.

In the close examination of turn designs of requesting, five major ways used to mark the request as delicate come to the fore: (1) deferring the request, (2) accounts, (3) appreciation, (4) indexing a distribution of benefits and/or costs associated with requesting and (5) the choice of

CHAPTER SEVEN CONCLUSION

imperatives, interrogatives and declaratives. Turn initial delays and designing other actions prior to the request proper are two practices to defer the initiation of requesting. Building accounts in the request turn reveals the requester's orientation toward the untowardness of requesting and legitimizes the request. In this way, a benefit-cost relationship is acknowledged. As for the benefit-cost relationship, this study shows that it can also be acknowledged by providing appreciation and indexing a distribution of benefits and/or costs associated with requesting respectively. Particular attention is also paid to practices (including minimal portrayal of requesting, minimization of costs of requesting to requestees and maximization of benefits of requesting to requesters) requesters use to index such a distribution. Minimal portrayal of requesting is achieved by avoidance or masqueraded requesting. The former normally gets a request successfully done without explicitly doing it, while the latter normally masquerades a request as other actions. Minimization of costs of requesting to requestees is achieved by selecting "softened" verbs characterized by brevity or by formatting the request as involving a minimal departure from requestees' routine. Maximization of benefits of requesting to requesters is accomplished by exaggerating the benefits for the requester than it really costs to the requestee. The last way involves the choice of imperatives, interrogatives and declaratives to initiate a request. These three lexical-syntactic formats which are positionally sensitive display how imposition of requesting on requestees is minimized.

In terms of interpretation of delicacy in requesting, this study shows that the choice of imperatives, interrogatives and declaratives to initiate a request is related to requesters' assessment of their entitlement to initiate the request and the contingency associated with the request to be granted, which is in line with Curl and Drew's findings (2008). The relation between entitlement/contingency and the lexical-syntactic formats of requesting displays the specific social norms constraining the choice of lexical-syntactic formats in doing requesting. It also shows that the requester's altruistic orientation can be observed in the practices exploited both in sequence organization and turn design of requesting when the requester initiates a request with the self-interested nature. The practices are social norms-governed. Social norms taken for granted by social members are the shared ways of behaving in a community. The social solidarity is achieved and maintained when people behave in the normative way, otherwise the solidary relation might be broken when social norms are neglected. The relationship among delicacy, altruism, social norms and social solidarity is reflexive. Altruism is the underlying engine for doing delicacy. Participants' orientation to social norms constructs delicacy in requesting and maintains social solidarity.

Contributions of the present study is summarized as follows:

To begin with, the theoretical contribution of the present study is the finding and generalization of goings-in-front-of-an-action and goings-in-front-of-requests, both of which provide us a better understanding of how one action, especially requesting is approached. Secondly, the study not only identifies and describes seen-but-unnoticed features of naturally occurring social interaction and generalizes the practices participants use to do requesting, but also interprets the mechanisms which underlie requesting. A detailed and dynamic picture of how requesting is organized is successfully presented from the perspective of sequence organization and turn design. Thirdly, it provides evidence for the argument that delicacy in requesting is interactionally produced and managed, rather than a pre-determined feature of requesting. Fourthly, it fills in the blanks about the reason why interrogatives and declaratives could be used to make requesting, which is never mentioned in traditional grammar and furthers our understanding about the connection between lexical-syntactic formats and the social action – requesting.

CHAPTER SEVEN CONCLUSION

7.2 Implications of the Present Study

    This study, theoretically speaking, provides an example for how to make an empirical investigation into social actions and enriches related studies. Taking Conversation Analysis as research methodology and through an intensive analysis of naturally occurring interaction as data, some new findings must be dug out.

    From the perspective of practical value, it sheds light on how to initiate a request appropriately, which maintains harmonious relationship between the requester and the requestee. It also sheds light on language pedagogy, especially Chinese as a foreign language. Teaching grammar based on studies on real-life conversations is of more importance and directive functions than those on idealized or fabricated ones. The present study may afford teachers lessons that pay attention to how co-participants do social actions by the target language in real-time conversations, e.g. to perform a request by imperatives or interrogatives, and incorporate interactions into teaching materials, as has been noticed that most of the dialogues in textbooks are unauthentic talks, which cannot display to the Chinese learners the actual use of language in natural conversations.

7.3 Limitations of the Present Study

    Though some findings and contributions have been achieved, there are still some limitations existing in the present study. Through an intensive analysis of the collected data, what drew my attention is delicacy displayed in requesting sequence. So attention is mainly paid to find out ways of initiating a request by the requester in which delicacy of requesting is demonstrated and to interpret why a request is presented in the way as it is, leaving aside some related points and other details. For instance, the relationship between the requester and the requestee might be at stake when a request is made, especially when a request gets rejected. But the question of how the relationship between the requester and the requestee is embodied, managed or reinforced in ways of the initiation of a request does not get an answer. As for the delicacy, for sake of space, attention is only paid to the requester who is the initiator of the requesting and how a request is initiated. But questions of how the requestee orients to the request, how the requestee makes a response, whether the requestee delicately treats the request and delicately designs his/her response and how the requester ends the request have not been analyzed.

7.4 Suggestions for Further Study

In the light of limitations, it needs a close study on the above-mentioned research questions to extend new findings of this study in the same direction of Conversation Analysis. There are other interesting research questions needs further investigating. The first one is accounts in requesting. As shown in the above analysis, sequential positions of accounts are flexible. What are the different interactional import of accounts placed in different sequential positions? Do accounts strengthen requesters' entitlement to make a request, as in Heinemann's findings (2006)? Are there any other functions besides accounting for requesting? All these questions need to be answered in future research. The second one is about requesting in diverse institutional settings. It is worthy of exploring whether all three lexical-syntactic formats, namely imperatives, interrogatives and declaratives are alternatives used to make requests in various institutional settings and whether requesting in these settings is treated as less delicate than in mundane conversations, for interactions in institutional settings are task-oriented and goal-driven (Drew &

CHAPTER SEVEN CONCLUSION

Heritage, 1992) and at least one party stands for the institution. The third one is about the scope of data. It can include interactions between children and adults, and children and children. Based on these interactions, research questions such as what factors play a role in children's socialization and how the asymmetric power balance (Wootton, 1981) between children and adults are displayed in requesting, etc. need investigating, which might contribute to a deeper understanding of children's socialization and a sound teaching methodology about preschool education. The fourth one is about requesting in face-to-face interactions. Because nonverbal ways such as eye contacts, nods, and body movements, etc. play an important role in the management of social interactions, it is also worthy of extending investigation on how requesting is formatted through multimodal resources and how these multimodal formats are organized in the request sequences, etc.

REFERENCES

Eglish Sources

Adelsward, V., Laughter and dialogue: The social significance of laughter in institutional discourse, *Nordic Journal of Linguistics*, 1989, 12 (2): 107 –136.

Aijmer, K., *Conversational Routines in English: Convention and Creativity*, London: Longman, 1996.

Akerlof, G. A., The economics of caste and of the rat race and other woeful tales, *Quarterly Journal of Economics*, 1976, 90 (4): 599 –617.

Alpe, Y., Lambert, J-R., Beitone, A., Dollo, C. & Parayre, S., *Lexique de Sociologie*, Paris: Dalloz, 2007.

Antaki, C. & Kent, A., Telling people what to do (and sometimes, why): Contingency, entitlement and explanation in staff requests to adults with intellectual impairments, *Journal of Pragmatics*, 2012, 44: 876 –889.

Atkinson, J. M. & Heritage, J. (Eds.), *Structures of Social Action: Studies in Conversation Analysis*, Cambridge, UK: Cambridge University Press, 1984.

Austin, J. L., *How to Do Thing with Words*, Oxford: Oxford University press, 1962.

Axelrod, R., An evolutionary approach to norms, *American Political Science Review*, 1986, 80 (4): 1095 –1111.

Baranova, J. & Dingemanse, M., Reasons for requests, *Discourse Studies*,

2016, 18 (6): 641 –675.

Barron, A., The structure of requests in Irish English and English English. In K. P. Schneider & A. Barron (Eds.), *Variational Pragmatics: A Focus on Regional Varieties of Pluricentric Languages*, Amsterdam/Philadelphia: John Benjamins. doi: 10. 1075/pbns. 178. 04bar, 2008, pp. 35 – 67.

Batson, C. D., *The Altruism Question: Toward a Social-psychological Answer*, Hillsdale, NJ: Lawrence Erlbaum Associates, 1991.

Batson, C. D., *Altruism in Humans*, New York: Oxford University Press, 2011.

Bayertz, K., Four uses of "solidarity", In K. Bayertz (Ed.), *Solidarity*, Dordrecht: Kluwer, 1999, pp. 3 – 28.

Beach, W. A., Transitional Regularities for Casual "Okay" Usages, *Journal of Pragmatics*, 1993, 19: 325 – 352.

Bergmann, J., Veiled morality: notes on discretion in psychiatry, In P. Drew & J. Heritage (Eds.), *Talk at Work*, Cambridge: Cambridge University Press, 1992, pp. 137 – 162.

Bierhoff, Hans-Werner, *Prosocial Behaviour*, New York: Taylor and Francis, 2002.

Blumer, H., Collective behavior, In R. E. Park (Ed.), *An Outline of the Principles of Sociology*, New York: Barnes & Noble, 1939, pp. 221 – 280.

Blum-Kulka, S., Playing it safe: The role of conventionality in indirectness, In S. Blum-Kulka, J. House & G. Kasper (Eds.), *Cross-Cultural Pragmatics: Requests and Apologies*, Norwood, NJ: Ablex, 1989, pp. 37 – 70.

Blum-Kulka, S., Danet, B. & Gherson, R., The language of requesting in Israeli society, In Joseph, F., (Ed.), *Language and Social Situation*, New York, Berlin: Springer, 1985, pp. 113 – 141.

Blum-Kulka, S. & House, J., "Cross-Cultural and situational variation in requesting behaviour", In S. Blum-Kulka, J. House, & G. Kasper (Eds.), *Cross-Cultural Pragmatics: Requests and Apologies*, Norwood, NJ: Ablex, 1989, pp. 123 – 154.

Blum-Kulka, S. & Olshtain, E., Requests and apologies: A cross-cultural study of speech act realization patterns, *Applied Linguistics*, 1984, 5: 196 – 213.

Blum-Kulka, S., House, J. & Kasper, G., *Cross-Cultural Pragmatics: Requests and Apologies*, Norwood, NJ: Ablex, 1989a.

Blum-Kulka, S., House, J. & Kasper, G., "Investigating cross cultural pragmatics: An introductory overview", In S. Blum-Kulka, J. House & G. Kasper (Eds.), *Cross-Cultural Pragmatics: Requests and Apologies*, Norwood, NJ: Ablex, 1989b, pp. 1 – 34.

Breuer, A. & Geluykens, R., Variation in British and American English requests: A contrastive analysis, In B. Kraft & R. Geluykens (Eds.), *Cross-Cultural Pragmatics and Interlanguage Pragmatics*, München: Lincom Europa, 2007, pp. 107 – 126.

Brown, P. & Levinson, S., Universals in language usage: politeness phenomena, In: Goody E. (Ed.), *Questions and Politeness: Strategies in Social Interaction*, Cambridge: Cambridge University Press, 1978, pp. 56 – 289.

Brown, P. & Levinson, S. C., *Politeness: Some Universals in Language Usage*, Cambridge: Cambridge University Press, 1987.

Clark, H. H. & Schunk, D. H., Polite responses to polite requests, *Cognition*, 1980, 8: 111 – 143.

Clayman, S. C., Footing in the achievement of neutrality: The case of news-interview discourse, In P. Drew & J. Heritage (Eds.), *Talk at Work*, Cambridge: Cambridge University Press, 1992, pp. 163 – 198.

Clayman, S. E., Sequence and solidarity, *Group Cohesion, Trust and Solidarity*, 2002, 19: 229 – 253.

Clayman, S. E., Turn-constructional units and the transition-relevance place,

REFERENCES

In J. Sidnell & T. Stivers (Eds.), *The Handbook of Conversation Analysis*, Oxford: Wiley-Blackwell, 2013, pp. 150 – 166.

Clayman, S. E. & Heritage, J., Benefactors and beneficiaires: Benefactive status and stance in the management of offers and requests, In P. Drew & E. Couper-Kuhlen (Eds.), *Requesting in social interaction*, Amsterdam: John Benjamins, 2014, pp. 55 – 86.

Clift, R., Drew, P. & Local, J., "Why that, now?": Position and composition in interaction (or, don't leave out the position in composition), In R. Kempson, C. Howes & M. Orwin (Eds.), *Language, Music and Interaction*, College Publications, 2013, pp. 211 – 232.

Comte, A., *System of Positive Polity*, (Vol. 1) London: Longmans, Green & Co., 1851.

Couper-Kuhlen, E., What does grammar tell us about action?, *Pragmatics*, 2014, 24 (3): 623 – 647.

Couper-Kuhlen, E. & Etelämäki, M., On divisions of labor in request and offer envionments, In P. Drew & E. Couper-Kuhlen (Eds.), *Requesting in social interaction*, Amsterdam: John Benjamins, 2014, pp. 115 – 144.

Couper-Kuhlen, E. & Etelämäki, M., Nominated actions and their targeted agents in Finnish conversational directives, *Journal of Pragmatics*, 2015, 78: 7 – 24.

Couper-Kuhlen, E., Fox, B. & Thompson, S. A., *Social Action Construction: Responding to Requests*, Presentation at the 12th International Pragmatics Conference, Manchester, UK, 4th July, 2011.

Craven, A. & Potter, J., Directives: entitlement and contingency in action, *Discourse Studies*, 2010, 12 (4): 419 – 442.

Cureton, A., Solidarity and social moral rules, *Ethical Theory and Moral Practice*, 2012, 15: 691 – 706.

Curl, T. S. & Drew, P., Contingency and action: a comparison of two forms of requesting, *Research on Language and Social Interaction*, 2008, 41

(2): 129 – 153.

Davidson, J., Subsequent versions of invitations, offers, requests, and proposals dealing with potential or actual rejection, In J. M. Atkinson & J. Heritage (Eds.), Structures of Social Action, *Studies in Conversation Analysis*, Cambridge: Cambridge University Press, 1984, pp. 102 – 128.

Dixon, S., Gimme! Gimme! Gimme!: Object requests, ownership and entitlement in a children's play session, *Journal of Pragmatics*, 2015, 82: 39 – 51.

Drew, P., Adult's corrections of children's mistakes, In P. French & M. MacLure (Eds.), *Adult-Child Conversations*, London: Croom Helm, 1981, pp. 244 – 267.

Drew, P., "Quit talking while I'm interrupting": A comparison between positions of overlap onset in conversation, In M. Haakana, M. Laakso & J. Lindström (Eds.), *Talk in Interaction: Comparative Dimensions*, Helsinki: Finnish Literature Society, 2010, pp. 70 – 93.

Drew, P., Conversation analysis and social action, *Journal of Foreign Languages*, 2013a, 36 (3): 2 – 19.

Drew, P., Turn design, In J. Sidnell and T. Stivers (Eds.), *The Handbook of Conversation Analysis*, Wiley-Blackwell, 2013b, pp. 57 – 76.

Drew, P. & Couper-Kuhlen, E., Requesting-from speech act to recruitment, In P. Drew & E. Couper-Kuhlen (Eds.), *Requesting in Social Interaction*, Amsterdam: John Benjamins, 2014, pp. 1 – 34.

Drew, P. & Heritage, J., Analyzing talk at work: an introduction, In P. Drew & J. Heritage (Eds.), *Talk at Work*, Cambridge, UK: Cambridge University Press, 1992, pp. 1 – 65.

Drew, P. & Heritage, J., *Talk at Work*, Cambridge, UK: Cambridge University Press, 1992.

Durkheim, E., *The Rules of Sociological Method*, New York: Palgrave MacMillan,

1895.

Durkheim, E., *The Rules of Sociological Method*, Glencoe, IL: The Free Press, 1950.

Economidou-Kogetsidis, M., Cross-cultural and situational variation in requesting behavior: perceptions of social situations and strategic usage of request patterns, *Journal of Pragmatics*, 2010, 42: 2262 – 2281.

Economidou-Kogetsidis, M., Strategies, modification and perspective in native speakers' requests: A comparison of WDCT and naturally occurring requests, *Journal of Pragmatics*, 53: 21 – 38. doi: 10.1016/j. pragma, 2013.03.014.

Editorial, Object requests: rights and obligations surrounding object possession and object transfer, *Journal of Pragmatics*, 2015, 82: 1 – 4.

Ellickson, R., *Order Without Law: How Neighbors Settle Disputes*, Cambridge: Harvard University Press, 1991.

Ellis, R., *The Study of Second Language Acquisition*, Oxford: Oxford University Press, 1994.

Enfield, N. J., Social consequences of common ground, In N. J. Enfield & S. C. Levinson (Eds.), *Roots of Human Sociality-Culture, Cognition and Interaction*, New York: Berg, 2006, pp. 399 – 430.

Enfield, N. J. & Sidnell, J., The normative nature of language, In N. Roughley & K. Bayertz (Eds.), *The Normative Animal? On the Anthropological Significance of Social, Moral, and Linguistic Norms*, New York: Oxford University Press, 2019, pp. 265 – 278.

Ervin-Tripp, S., Is Sybil there? The structure of some American English directives, *Language in Society*, 1976, 5 (1): 25 – 66.

Ervin-Tripp, S., Wait for me, roller skake, In S. Ervin-Tripp & C. Mitchelle-Kernan (Eds.), *Child Discourse*, New York: Academic Press, 1977, pp. 165 – 188.

Faerch, C. & Kasper, G., Internal and External Modification in Interlanguage

Request Realization, In S. Blum-Kulka, J. House & G. Kasper (Eds.), *Cross-Cultural Pragmatics: Requests and Apologies*, Norwood, NJ: 1989, pp. 221 – 247.

Felix-Brasderfer, J. C., Indirectness and politeness in Mexican requests, In Eddinton, D. (Ed.), *Selected Proceedings of the 7th Hispanic Linguistics Symposium*, Somerville, MA: Cascadilla Proceedings Project, 2005, pp. 66 – 78.

Flöck, I., *Requests in American and British English: A Contrastive Multi-method Analysis*, Amsterdan/Philadelphia: John Benjamins Publishing Company, 2016.

Foote, N., Identification as the basis for a theory of motivation, *American Sociological Review*, 1951, 16: 14 – 21.

Ford, C. E. & Thompson, S. A., Interactional units in conversation: Syntactic, intonation and pragmatic resources for the management of turns, In E. Ochs, E. A. Schegloff & S. A. Thompson (Eds.), *Interaction and Grammar*, Cambridge: Cambridge University Press, 1996, pp. 134 – 184.

Fukushima, S., Request strategies in British English and Japanese, *Language Sciences*, 1996, 18 (3 – 4): 671 – 688.

Fukushima, S., *Requests and Culture: Politeness in British English and Japanese*, Bern: Peter Lang, 2000.

Gao, H., Features of request strategies in Chinese, *Working Papers*, 1999, 47: 73 – 86. http://www.ling.lu.se/disseminations/pdf/47/Gao.pdf.

Garfinkel, H., *Studies in Ethnomethodology*, Englewood Cliffs, NJ: Prentice-Hall, 1967.

Geertz, C., *Thick Description: Toward an Interpretive Theory of Culture in The Interpretation of Cultures: Selected Essays*, New York: Basic Books, 1973.

Gibbs, R. W., Your wish is my command: Convention and context in interpreting indirect requests, In Kasper, ASA. (Ed.), *Pragmatics-Critical Concepts, VI: Pragmatics: Grammar, Psychology and Sociology*, Routledge, 1998.

REFERENCES

Goffman, E., On face-work: An analysis of ritual elements in social interaction, *Psychology*, 1955, 18: 213 – 231.

Goffman, E., *The Presentation of Self in Everyday Life*, Garden City, NY: Anchor, 1959.

Goffman, E., *Interaction Ritual*: Essays in Face to Face Behavior, Garden City, NY: Doubleday, 1967.

Goffman, E., *Relations in Public*, Microstudies of the Public Order, New York: Basic Books, 1971.

Goffman, E., Response cries, In E. Goffman (Ed.), *Forms of Talk*, Oxford: Blackwell, 1981, pp. 78 – 122.

Goffman, E., The interaction order: American sociological association, 1982 presidential address, *American Sociological Review*, 1983, 48 (1): 1 – 17.

Goodwin, M. H. & Cekaite, A., Orchestrating directive trajectories in communicative projects in family interaction, In P. Drew & E. Couper-Kuhlen (Eds.), *Requesting in Social Interaction*, Amsterdam: John Benjamins, 2014, pp. 185 – 214.

Green, G. M., How to get people to do things with words: The whimperative question, In P. Cole & J. L. Morgan (Eds.), *Syntax and Semantics 3*: *Speech Acts*, New Yor: Academic Press, 1975, pp. 107 – 141.

Haakana, M., Laughter as a patient's resource: Dealing with delicate aspects of medical interaction, *Text*, 2001, 21 (1/2): 187 – 219.

Haakana, M., Laughter and smiling: notes on co-occurences, *Journal of Pragmatics*, 2010, 42 (6): 1499 – 1512.

Hayano, K., Question design in conversation, In J. Sidnell & T. Stivers (Eds.), *The Handbook of Conversation Analysis*, Wiley-Blackwell, 2013, pp. 395 – 414.

Hayashi, M., Turn allocation and turn sharing, In J. Sidnell & T. Stivers (Eds.), *The Handbook of Conversation Analysis*, Wiley-Blackwell, 2012, pp. 167 – 190.

Heath, C. & Luff, P., Explicating face-to-face interaction, In N. Gilbert (Ed.), *Researching Social Life*, London: Sage, 1993, pp. 306 – 326.

Heath, C., Embarrassment and interactional organization, In P. Drew & A. Wootton (Eds.), *Erving Goffman: Exploring the Interaction Order*, Cambridge: Polity Press, 1988, pp. 136 – 150.

Hechter, M. & Opp, K.-D., *Social Norms*, New York: Russel Sage Foundation, 2001.

Heinemann, T., "Will you or can't you?": Displaying entitlement in interrogative requests, *Journal of Pragmatics*, 2006, 38: 1082 – 1104.

Hepburn, A. & Bolden, G. B., The conversation analytic approach to transcription, In J. Sidnell & T. Stivers (Eds.), *The Handbook of Conversation Analysis*, West Sussex, UK: Wiley-Blackwell, 2013, pp. 57 – 76.

Heritage, J., Explanations as accounts: a conversation analytic perspective, In C. Antaki (Ed.), *Analyzing Everyday Explanation: A Casebook of Methods*, London: Sage Publications Ltd., 1988, pp. 127 – 144.

Heritage, J., Conversation analysis and institutional talk: Analysing data, In D. Sliverman (Ed.), *Qualitative Research: Theory, Method and Practice*, London: Sage, 1997, pp. 161 – 182.

Heritage, J., Epistemics in action: Action formation and territories of knowledge, *Research on Language and Social Interaction*, 2012, 45: 1 – 25.

Heritage, J. & Clayman, S., *Talk in Action: Interactions, Identities and Institutions*, Wiley-Blackwell, 2010.

Heritage, J. & Sorjonen M.-L., Constituting and maintaining activities across sequences: And-prefacing as a feature of question design, *Language in Society*, 1994, 23 (1): 1 – 29.

Heritage, J. & Watson, D. R., Formulations as Conversational Objects, In G. Psathas (Ed.), *Everyday Language*, New York: Irvington Press,

REFERENCES

1979, pp. 123 – 162.

Heritage, J., *Garfinkel and Ethnomethodology*, Cambridge, MA: Polity Press, 1984a.

Heritage, J., A change-of-state token and aspects of its sequential placement, In J. M. Atkinson & J. Heritage (Eds.), *Structures of Social Action: Studies in Conversation Analysis*, Cambridge: Cambridge University Press, 1984b, pp. 299 – 345.

Hill, B., Ide, S., Ikuta, S., Kawasaki, A. & Ogino, T., Universals of linguistic politeness: quantitative evidence from Japanese and American English, *Journal of Pragmatics*, 1986, 10 (3): 347 – 371.

Hoey, E. & Kendrick, K. H., Conversation analysis, In A. M. B. de Groot & P. Hagoort (Eds.), *Research Methods in Psycholinguistics and The Neurobiology Of Language: A Practical Guide*, Hoboken: Wiley, 2018, pp. 151 – 173.

Holt, E., Reporting and reacting: Concurrent responses to reported speech, *Research on Language and Social Interaction*, 2000, 33 (4): 425 – 454.

Holtgraves, T. & Yang, J., Politeness as universal: cross-cultural perceptions of request strategies and inferences based on their use, *Journal of Personality and Social Psychology*, 1990, 59 (4): 719 – 729.

House, J. & Kasper, G., Politeness markers in English and German, In F. Coulmas (Ed.), *Conversational Routine: Explorations in Standardized Communication Situations and Prepatterned Speech*, The Hague: Mouton, 1981, pp. 157 – 185.

Huang, M. -C., *Achieving Cross-cultural Equivalence in a Study of American and Taiwanese Requests*, PhD diss., University of Illinois, 1996.

Hunt, S., *Constructing Collective Identity in a Peace Movement Organization* (PhD dissertation), University of Nebraska, 1991.

Hutchby, I. & Wooffitt, R., *Conversation Analysis: Principles, Practices and Applications*, Cambridge: Polity Press, 1998.

Jefferson, G., Side sequences, In D. Sudnow (Ed.), *Studies in Social Interaction*, New York: Free Press, 1972, pp. 294 – 338.

Jefferson, G., Notes on some orderliness of overlap onset, In V. D'Urso & P. Leonardi (Eds.), *Discourse Analysis and Natural Rhetoric*, Padua: Cleup Editore, 1983, pp. 11 – 38.

Jefferson, G., On stepwise transition from talk about a trouble to inappropriately next-positioned matters, In J. M. Atkinson & J. Heritage (Eds.), *Structures of Social Action: Studies in Conversation Analysis*, Cambridge, UK: Cambridge University Press, 1984a, pp. 191 – 222.

Jefferson, G., Notes on some orderlinesses of overlap onset, In V. D'Urso & P. Leonardi (Eds.), *Discourse Analysis and Natural Rhetoric*, Padua: Cleup Editore, 1984b, pp. 11 – 38.

Jefferson, G., An Eexercise in the Transcription and Analysis of Laughter, In T. A. Dijk (Ed.), *Handbook of Discourse Analysis vol. 3*, New York: Academic Press, 1985, pp. 25 – 34.

Jefferson, G., On the sequential organization of troubles talk in ordinary conversation, *Social Problems*, 1988, 35 (4): 418 – 441.

Jordan, B. & Henderson, A., Interaction Analysis: Foundations and Practice, *The Journal of the Learning Sciences*, 1995, 4: 39 – 101.

Keisanen, T. & Rauniomaa, M., The organization of participant and contingency in prebeginnings of request sequences, *Research on Language and Social Interaction*, 2012, 45 (4): 323 – 351.

Kendrick, K. H. & Drew, P., The putative preference for offers over requests, In P. Drew & E. Couper-Kuhlen (Eds.), *Requesting in Social Interaction*, Amsterdam: John Benjamins, 2014, pp. 87 – 113.

Kendrick, K. H. & Drew, P., Recruitment: offers, requests, and the organization of assistance in interaction, *Research on Language and Social Interaction*, 2016, 49 (1): 1 – 19.

Lakoff, R., What you can to do with words: politeness, pragmatics and performatives, In A. Rogers, B. Wall & J. P. Murphy (Eds.), *Proceedings of the Texas Conference on Performatives, Presuppositions and Implicature*, Washington, DC: Center for Applied Linguistics, 1977, pp. 79 –105.

Larkin, D. & O'Malley, M. H., Declarative sentences and the rule-of-conversation hypothesis, *Papers from the Ninth Regional Meeting of the Chicago Linguistic Society*, Chicago, 1973: 306 – 319.

Leech, G., *Principles of Pragmatics*, London: Longman, 1983.

Lee-Wong, S. M., *Politeness and Face in Chinese Culture: Cross Cultural Communication*, Melbourne: Monash University Press, 2000.

Lee-Wong, S. M., Imperatives in requests: direct or impolite: observations from Chinese, *Pragmatics*, 1994, 4 (4): 491 –515.

Lerner, G. H., On the place of hesitating in delicate formulations: a turn-constructional infrastructure for collaborative indiscretion, In M. Hayashi, G. Raymond & J. Sidnell (Eds.), *Conversation Repair and Human Understanding*, Cambridge: Cambridge University Press, 2013, pp. 95 – 134.

Lerner, G. H. (Ed.), *Conversation Analysis: Studies From the First Generation*, Amsterdam/Philadelphia: John Benjamins, 2004.

Levinson, S. C., *Pragmatics*, Cambridge: Cambridge University Press, 1983.

Levinson, S. C., Interrogative intimations: on a possible social economics of interrogatives, In J. P. de Ruiter (Ed.), *Questions: Formal, Functional and Interactional Perspectives*, Cambridge: Cambridge University Press, 2012, pp. 11 – 32.

Li, Charles N. & Thompson, S. A., *Mandarin Chinese: A Functional Reference Grammar*, Los Angeles: University of California Press, 1989.

Li, Li & Ma, Wen, Request sequence in Chinese public service calls, *Discourse Studies*, 2016, 18 (3): 269 – 285.

Liao Chao-chih, *A Contrastive Study of Chinese and English Directive*, Unpublished

MA thesis. National Taiwan Normal University, 1982.

Liao Chao-chih, *Comparing Directives: American English, Mandarin and Taiwanese English*, The Crane Publishing Co., Ltd., 1997.

Lin, Yuh-Huey, Query preparatory modals: Cross-linguistic and cross-situational variations in request modification, *Journal of Pragmatics*, 2009, 41 (8): 1636 – 1656. doi: 10.1016/j. pragma, 2008.12.007

Lindström, A., Language as social action: A study of how senior citizens request assistance with practical tasks in the Swedish home help service, In A. Hakulinen & M. Selting (Eds.), *Syntax and Lexis in Conversation Studies on the use of linguisticresources in talk-in-interaction*, Amsterdam/Philadelphia: John Benjamins Publishing Company, 2005, pp. 209 – 230.

Linell, P. & Bredmar, M., Reconstructing topical sensitivity: Aspects of face-work in talks between midwives and expectant mothers, *Research on Language and Social Interaction*, 1996, 29 (4): 347 – 379.

Lyons, J., *Introduction to Theoretical Linguistics*, Cambridge: Cambridge University Press, 1968.

Lyons, J., *Semantics*, Cambridge: Cambridge University Press, 1977.

Macaulay, J. R. & Berkowitz, L. (Eds.), *Altruism and Helping Behavior*, New York: Academic Press, 1970.

Mandelbaum, J., How to do things with requests: Request sequences at the family dinner table, In P. Drew & E. Couper-Kuhlen (Eds.), *Requesting in Social Interaction*, Amsterdam: John Benjamins, 2014, pp. 215 – 241.

Marti, L., Indirectness and politeness in Turkish-German bilingual and Turkish monolingual requests, *Journal of Pragmatics*, 2006, 38 (11): 1836 – 1869.

Maynard, D., Interaction and asymmetry in clinical discourse, *American Journal of Sociology*, 1991, 97 (2): 448 – 495.

Melucci, A., *Challenging Codes: Collective Action in the Information Age*,

REFERENCES

New York: Cambridge University Press, 1996.

Mondada, L., The Conversation Analytic Approach to Data Collection, In J. Sidnell & T. Stivers (Eds.), *The Handbook of Conversation Analysis*, Wiley-Blackwell, 2013, pp. 32 - 56.

Mondada, L., Requesting immediate action in the surgical operating room: Time, embodied resources and praxeological embeddedness, In P. Drew & E. Couper-Kuhlen (Eds.), *Requesting in Social Interaction*, Amsterdam: John Benjamins, 2014, pp. 269 - 302.

Ogiermann, E., Politeness and in-directness across cultures: A comparison of English, German, Polish and Russian requests, *Journal of Politeness Research*, 2009, 5: 189 - 216. doi: 10.1515/JPLR.2009.011.

Ogiermann, E., In/directness in Polish children's requests at the diner table, *Journal of Pragmatics*, 2015, 82: 67 - 82.

Oliner, S. P. & Oliner, P. M., *The altruistic personality: Rescuers of Jews in Nazi Europe*, New York: The Free Press, 1988.

Pan, Yuling, *Politeness Strategies in Chinese Verbal Interaction: A Sociolinguistic Analysis of Spoken Data in Official, Business and Family Settings*, Washington, DC: Georgetown University, 1994.

Parsons, T. & Shils, E. A., *Towards a General Theory of Action*, Cambridge, MA: Harvard University Press, 1951.

Parsons, T., *The Structure of Social Action. A Study in Social Theory with Special Reference to a Group of Recent European Writers*, New York, London: Free Press, 1937.

Pomerantz, A., Agreeing and disagreeing with assessments: Some features of preferred/dispreferred turn shape, In J. M. Atkinson & J. Heritage (Eds.), *Structures of Social Action: Studies in Conversation Analysis*, Cambridge, UK: Cambridge University Press, 1984, pp. 57 - 101.

Pomerantz, A., Extreme case formulations: A way of legitimizing claims, *Human Studies*, 1986, 9 (2 - 3): 219 - 229.

Pomerantz, A. & Heritage, J., Preference, In J. Sidnell & T. Stivers (Eds.), *The Handbook of Conversation Analysis*, West Sussex, UK: Wiley-Blackwell, 2013, pp. 210 – 228.

Popitz, H., Social norms, *Genocide Studies and Prevention: An International Journal*, 2017, 11 (2): 3 – 12.

Posner, E., *Law and Social Norms*, Harvard University Press, 2000.

Post, S. G., Six sources of altruism: Springs of morality and solidarity, In V. Jeffries (Ed.), *The Palgrave Handbook of Altruism, Morality, and Social Solidarity*, NY: Palgrave Macmillan, 2014, pp. 179 – 193.

Psathas, G., *Conversation Analysis: the Study of Talk-in-Interaction*, Thousand Oaks, California: Sage, 1995.

Psathas, G. (Ed), *International Competence*, Washington, DC: University Press of America, 1990.

Rauniomaa, M. & Keisanen, T., Two multimodal formats for responding to requests, *Journal of Pragmatices*, 2012, 44: 829 – 842.

Raymond, G., Grammar and social organization: Yes/no interrogatives and the structure of responding, *American Sociological Review*, 2003, 68: 939 – 967.

Reiter, R. M., *Linguistic Politeness in Britain and Uruguay: A Contrastive Study of Requests and Apologies*, Amsterdam: John Benjamins, 2000.

Revillard, A., Social norms (1): norms and deviance: Introduction to sociology-session 2. Unpublished, 2019.

Robinson, J. D. & Bolden, G. B., Preference organization of sequence-initiating actions: The case of explicit account solicitations, *Discourse Studies*, 2010, 12: 501 – 533.

Rossano, F. & Liebal, K. "Requests" and "offers" in orangutans and human infants, In P. Drew & E. Couper-Kuhlen (Eds.), *Requesting in Social Interaction*, Amsterdam: John Benjamins, 2014, pp. 335 – 363.

Rossi, G., Bilateral and unilateral requests: the use of imperatives and *Mi*

X? interrogatives in Italian, *Discourse Process*, 2012, 49: 426 – 458.

Rossi, G., Responding to pre-requests: The organization of *hai x* "do you have x" sequences in Italian, *Journal of Pragmatics*, 2015, 82: 5 – 22.

Rue, Y. & Zhang, G., *Request Strategies: A Comparative Study in Mandarin Chinese and Korean*, Amsterdam, Philadelphia: John Benjamins Publishing Company, 2008.

Sacks, H., The search for help: No one to turn to, In E. Schneidman (Ed.), *Essays in Self-destruction*, New York: Science House, 1972a, pp. 203 – 223.

Sacks, H., *The Search for Help: No One to Turn to*, Unpublished PhD Dissertation. Berkeley, University of California, 1972b.

Sacks, H., On the preferences for agreement and contiguity in sequences in conversation, In G. Button & J. R. Lee (Eds.), *Talk and Social Organisation* Clevedon, England: Multilingual Matters, 1987, pp. 54 – 69.

Sacks, H., *Lectures on Conversation Analysis*, Vol. I. Edited by G. Jefferson with an introduction by E. A. Schegloff, Oxford: Basil Blackwell, 1992a.

Sacks, H., Lectures on Conversation Analysis, Vol. II. Edited by G. Jefferson with an introduction by E. A. Schegloff, Oxford: Basil Blackwell, 1992b.

Sacks, H., Schegloff, E. & Jefferson, G., A simplest systematics for the organization of turn-taking for conversation, *Language*, 1974, 50 (4): 696 – 735.

Schegloff, E. A., Sequencing in Conversational Openings, *American Anthropologist*, 1968, 70 (6): 1075 – 1095.

Schegloff, E. A., Notes on a conversational practice: Formulating place, In D. Sudnow (Ed.), *Studies in Social Interaction*, New York: Free Press, 1972, pp. 75 – 119.

Schegloff, E. A., Preliminaries to preliminaries: "Can I Ask You a Question?", *Sociological Inquiry*, 1980, 50 (3-4): 104 – 152.

Schegloff, E. A., The routine as achievement, *Human Studies*, 1986, 9:

111 – 151.

Schegloff, E. A., On an actual virtual servo-mechanism for guessing bad news: A single case conjecture, *Social Problems*, 1988, 35 (4): 442 – 57.

Schegloff, E. A., Sequence as a source of coherence in conversation, In B. Dorval (Ed.), *Conversational Organization and Its Development*, Norwood, NJ: Ablex Publishing, 1990, pp. 111 – 151.

Schegloff, E. A., Reflections on talk and social structure, In D. Boden & D. H. Zimmerman (Eds.), *Talk and Social Structure: Studies in Ethnomethodology and Conversation Analysis*, Cambridge: Polity Press, 1991, pp. 44 – 71.

Schegloff, E. A., *Sequence Organization In Interaction: A Primer In Conversation Analysis*, Cambridge: Cambridge University Press, 2007.

Schegloff, E. A., Some other u(h)ms, *Discourse Processes*, 2010, 47 (2): 130 – 174.

Schegloff, E. A. & Sacks, H., Opening up closings, *Semiotica*, 1973, 8: 289 – 327.

Scholz, S., *Political Solidarity*, University Park: The Pennsylvania State University Press, 2008.

Scott, M. B. & Lyman, S. M., Accounts, *American Sociological Review*, 1968, 33 (1): 46 – 62.

Searle, J. R., *Speech Acts: An Essay in the Philosophy of Language*, Cambridge: Cambridge University Press, 1969.

Searle, J. R., The classification of illocutionary acts, *Language in Society*, 1976, 5 (1): 1 – 24.

Searle, J. R., *Expression and Meaning: Studies in the Theory of Speech Acts*, Cambridge: Cambridge University Press, 1979.

Searle, J. R. & Vanderveken, D., *Foundations of Illocutionary Logic*, Cambridge: Cambridge University Press, 1985.

Sidenell, J., *Conversation Analysis an Introduction*, Oxford: Wiley-Blackwell,

2010.

Sidenell, J., Basic conversation analytic methods, In J. Sidnell & T. Stivers (Eds.), *The Handbook of Conversation Analysis*, Wiley-Blackwell, 2013, pp. 77 – 99.

Sifianou, M., *Politeness Phenomena in England and Greece: A Cross-cultural Perspective*, Oxford: Oxford University Press, 1992.

Sigman, S. J., *The Consequential of Communication*, London; New York: Routledge, 1995.

Silverman, D., *Communication and Medical Practice: Social Relations in the Clinic*, London: Sage, 1987.

Silverman, D., *Discourses of Counselling: HIV Counselling as Social Interaction*, London: Sage, 1997.

Silverman, D., The construction of "delicate" objects in counseling, In M. Wetherell, S. Taylor & S. J. Yates (Eds.), *Discourse Theory and Practice-A Reader*, London: Sage Publications, 2001, pp. 119 – 137.

Silverman, D. & Peräkylä, A., AIDS counselling: the interactional organisation of talk about "delicate" issues, *Sociology of Health and Illness*, 1990, 12 (3): 293 – 318.

Skyrms, B., *Evolution of the Social Contract*, Cambridge University Press, 1996.

Smith, C. & Sorrell, K., On social solidarity, In V. Jeffries (Ed.), *The Palgrave Handbook of Altruism, Morality and Social Solidarity*, New York: Palgrave Macmillan, 2014, pp. 219 – 247.

Sorjonen, M. & Raevaara, L., On the grammatical form requests at the convenience store: Requesting as embodied action, In P. Drew & E. Couper-Kuhlen (Eds.), *Requesting in Social Interaction*, Amsterdam: John Benjamins, 2014, pp. 243 – 268.

Steensig, J. & Heinemann, T., The social and moral work of modal constructions in granting remote requests, In P. Drew & E. Couper-Kuhlen (Eds.),

Requesting in Social Interaction, Amsterdam: John Benjamins, 2014, pp. 145 – 170.

Stevanovic, M., Participants' deontic rights and action formation: the case of declarative requests for action, *In LiSt Interact. Linguist. Struct*, 2011, 52, http://www.inlist.uni-bayreuth.de/.

Stivers, T., Introduction, In J. Sidnell & T. Stivers (Eds.), The Handbook of Conversation Analysis, Wiley-Blackwell, 2013, pp. 191 – 209.

Stivers, T. & Sidnell, S., Introduction, In J. Sidnell & T. Stivers (Eds.), *The Handbook of Conversation Analysis*, Wiley-Blackwell, 2013, pp. 1 – 8.

Stubbs, M., *Discourse Analysis – The Sociolinguistic Analysis of Natural Language*, Oxford: Blackwell, 1983.

Suoninen, E., Doing delicacy in institutions of helping: a case of probation office interaction, In A. Jokinen, K. Juhila & T. Pösö (Eds.), *Constructing Social Work Practices*, Aldershot: Ashgate, 1999, pp. 103 – 115.

Takada, A. & Endo, T., Object transfer in request-accept sequence in Japanese caregiver-child interactions, *Journal of Pragmatics*, 2015, 82: 52 – 66.

Taleghani-Nikazm, C., Contingent requests: their sequential organization and turn shape, *Research on Language and Social Interaction*, 2005, 38 (2): 159 – 177.

Taleghani-Nikazm, C., *Request Sequences: The Intersection of Grammar, Interaction and Social Context*, Amsterdam; Philadelphia, PA: John Benjamins Publishing Company, 2006.

ten Have, P., *Doing Conversation Analysis: A practical Guide* (2nd ed.), London: Sage, 2007.

Thomas, J., Cross-cultural pragmatic failure, *Applied Linguistics*, 1983, 4: 91 – 112.

Tiryakian, E. A. & Morgan, J. H., Solidarity, yesterday and today, In V. Jeffries (Ed.), *The Palgrave Handbook of Altruism, Morality and*

Social Solidarity, New York: Palgrave Macmillan, 2014, pp. 249 – 271.

Triandafillides, M., *Neolliniki Grammatiki* (*tis dimotikis*), Rev. edn. (Aristotelio Panepistimio Thessalonikis), 1978.

Trosborg, A., *Interlanguage Pragmatics: Requests, Complaints, and Apologies*, Berlin: Mouton de Gruyter, 1995.

Tsui, A., *English Conversation*, 上海: 上海外语出版社, 2000.

Ullmann-Margalit, E., *The Emergence of Norms*, Oxford: Clarendon Press, 1977.

van Nijnatten, C. & Suoninen, E., Delicacy, In C. Hall, K. J., M. Matarese & C. van Nijnatten (Eds.), *Analyzing Social Work Communication: Discourse in Practice*, London & New York: Routledge Taylor & Francis Group, 2014, pp. 136 – 153.

Vinkhuyzen, E. & Hzymanski, M. H., Would you like to do it yourself? Service requests and their non-granting responses, In K. Richards & P. Seedhouse (Eds.), *Applying Conversation Analysis*, New York: Palgrave Macmillan, 2005, pp. 91 – 106.

Voloshinov, V. N., Reported speech, In L. Matejka & K. Promorska (Eds.), *Readings in Russian Poetics: Formalist and Structuralist Views*, Cambridge, MA: MIT Press, 1971, pp. 149 – 175.

Walker, T., Drew, P. & Local, J., Responding indirectly, *Journal of Pragmatics*, 2011, 43: 2434 – 2451.

Wardhaugh, R., *How Conversation Works*, Oxford: Blackwell, 1985.

Weijts, W. Houtkoop, H. & Mullen, P., Talking delicacy: Speaking about sexuality during gynaecological consultations, *Sociology of Health and Illness*, 1993, 15 (3): 295 – 314.

Wilson, D. S., *Does Altruism Exist?: Culture, Genes, and the Welfare of Others*, New Haven and London: Yale University Press, 2015.

Wootton, A. J., The management of grantings and rejections by parents in request sequences, *Semiotica*, 1981, 37: 59 – 90.

Wootton, A. J., *Interaction and development of mind*, Cambridge, England: Cambridge University Press, 1997.

Wootton, A. J., Interactional and Sequential Configurations Informing Request Format Selection in Children's Speech, In A. Hakulinen & M. Selting (Eds.), *Syntax and Lexis in Conversation Studies on the use of linguistic resources in talk-in-interaction*, Amsterdam/Philadelphia: John Benjamins Publishing Company, 2005, pp. 185 – 207.

Young, H. P., Social norms and economic welfare, *European Economic Review*, 1998, 42: 821 – 830.

Yu, Guodong & Drew, P., The role of búshì (不是) in talk about everyday troubles and difficulties, *East Asian Pragmatics*, 2017, 2 (2): 195 – 227.

Yu, Guodong & Wu, Yaxin, Managing awkward, sensitive, or delicate topics in (Chinese) radio medical consultations, *Discourse Processes*, 2015, 52: 201 – 225.

Yu, Guodong., Establishing solidarity in radio phone-in medical consultation in China-A case study, *Journal of Asian Pacific Communication*, 2010, 20 (2): 226 – 242.

Zhang, Y., Strategies in Chinese requesting, In G. Kasper (Ed.), *Pragmatics of Chinese as Native and Target Language*, Honolulu, HI: University of Hawai'i at Manoa, Second Language Teaching and Curriculum Centre, 1995, pp. 23 – 68.

Zinken, J., Contingent control over shared goods, "Can I have x" requests in British English informal interaction, *Journal of Pragmatics*, 2015, 82: 23 – 38.

Zinken, J. & Ogiermann, E., Responsibility and Action: Invariants and Diversity in Requests for Objects in British English and Polish Interaction, *Research on Language and Social Interaction*, 2013, 46 (3): 256 – 276.

Zinken, J. & Rossi, G., Assistance and other forms of cooperative engagement,

Research on Language and Social Interaction, 2016, 49(1): 20-26.

中文文献

范杏丽:《汉语请求策略研究:一项基于跨文化视角的对比》,博士学位论文,上海外国语大学,2011年。

贾少敏:《概念整合理论下间接请求言语行为的转喻研究》,硕士学位论文,辽宁师范大学,2011年。

鞠志勤:《认知视角下的请求言语行为研究》,硕士学位论文,山东大学,2007年。

刘陈艳:《中国英语学习者请求言语行为的语用研究——基于非英语专业大学生的语料》,博士学位论文,上海外国语大学,2014年。

刘国辉:《英汉请求策略理论与实证对比研究》,博士学位论文,复旦大学,2003年。

刘蜀、于国栋:《汉语言语交际中前序列与前序序列的会话分析研究——以请求行为为例》,《外语教学》2018年第2期。

任伟:《汉语请求言语行为的变异语用学研究》,《外国语》2018年第4期。

王晓彤:《影响汉语请求言语行为的社会变量研究》,博士学位论文,东北师范大学,2012年。

吴亚欣、杨永芳:《汉语日常会话中序列结束语"好吧"的会话分析》,《语言学研究》2020年第1期。

杨仙菊:《第二语言语用习得:中国学习者英语"请求"言语行为习得的横向研究》,博士学位论文,上海外国语大学,2006年。

于国栋:《请求作为伤面子行为的会话佐证》,《北京第二外国语学院学报》2019年第4期。

张绍杰、王晓彤:《"请求"言语行为的对比研究》,《现代外语》1997年第3期。

APPENDIX
TRANSCRIPTION CONVENTIONS

I. Temporal and sequential relationships

Overlapping or simultaneous talk is indicated in a variety of ways.

[ ]	Separate left square brackets, one above the other on two successive lines with utterances by different speakers, indicate a point of overlap onset, whether at the start of an utterance or later.
]]	Separate right square brackets, one above the other on two successive lines with utterances by different speakers, indicate a point at which two overlapping utterances both end or where one ends while the other continues, or simultaneous moments in overlaps which continue.
=	Equal signs ordinarily come in pairs, one at the end of a line, and another at the start of the next line or one shortly thereafter. They are used to indicate two things: (1) If the two lines connected by the equal signs are by the same speaker, then there was a single, continuous utterance with no break or pause, which was broken up in order to accommodate the placement of overlapping talk. (2) If the lines connected by two equal signs are by different speakers, then the second followed the first with no discernible silence between them, or was "latched" to it.
(0.5)	Numbers in parentheses indicate silence, represented in tenths of a second; what is given here in the left margin indicates 0.5 seconds of silence. Silences may be marked either within an utterance or between utterances.
(.)	A dot in parentheses indicates a "micropause", hearable, but not readily measurable without instrumentation; ordinarily less than 0.2 of a second.

II. Aspects of speech delivery, including aspects of intonation

. ? , ¿	The punctuation marks are not used grammatically, but to indicate intonation. The period indicates a falling, or final, intonation contour, not necessarily the end of a sentence. Similarly, a question mark indicates rising intonation, not necessarily a question, and a comma indicates "continuing" intonation, not necessarily a clause boundary. The inverted question mark is used to indicate a rise stronger than a comma but weaker than a question mark.

APPENDIX TRANSCRIPTION CONVENTIONS

: :	Colons are used to indicate the prolongation or stretching of the sound just preceding them. The more colons, the longer the stretching. On the other hand, graphically stretching a word on the page by inserting blank spaces between the letters does not necessarily indicate how it was pronounced; it is used to allow alignment with overlapping talk.
-	A hyphen after a word or part of a word indicates a cut-off or self-interruption, often done with a glottal or dental stop.
w<u>o</u>rd	Underlining is used to indicate some form of stress or emphasis, by either increased loudness or higher pitch. The more underlining, the greater the emphasis.
<u>w</u>ord	Therefore, underlining sometimes is placed under the first letter or two of a word, rather than under the letters which are actually raised in pitch or volume.
WOrd	Especially loud talk may be indicated by upper case; again, the louder, the more letters in upper case. And in extreme cases, upper case may be underlined.
° °word°	The degree sign indicates that the talk following it is markedly quiet or soft. When there are two degree signs, the talk between them is markedly softer than the talk around it.
_: :̲	Combinations of underlining and colons are used to indicate intonation contours: If the letter (s) preceding a colon is (are) underlined, then there is an "inflected" falling intonation contour on the vowel (you can hear the pitch turn downward). If a colon is itself underlined, then there is an inflected rising intonation contour.
↑ or ˆ ↓	The up and down arrows mark sharper rises or falls in pitch than would be indicated by combinations of colons and underlining, or they may mark a whole shift, or resetting, of the pitch register at which the talk is being produced.
> < < >	The combination of "more than" and "less than" symbols indicates that the talk between them is compressed or rushed. Used in the reverse order, they can indicate that a stretch of talk is markedly slowed or drawn out. The "less than" symbol by itself indicates that the immediately following talk is "jump-started", i.e. sounds like it starts with a rush.
hhh (hh) °hh °hh	Hearable aspiration is shown where it occurs in the talk by the letter h - the more h's, the more aspiration. The aspiration may represent breathing, laughter, etc. If it occurs inside the boundaries of a word, it may be enclosed in parentheses in order to set it apart from the sounds of the word. If the aspiration is an inhalation, it is shown with a dot before it (usually a raised dot) or a raised degree symbol.

III. Other markings

(( ))	Double parentheses are used to mark the transcriber's descriptions of events, rather than representations of them: ((cough)), ((sniff)), ((telephone rings)), ((footsteps)), ((whispered)), ((pause)), and the like.
(word)	When all or part of an utterance is in parentheses, or the speaker identification is, this indicates uncertainty on the transcriber's part, but represents a likely possibility.
( )	Empty parentheses indicate that something is being said, but no hearing (or, in some cases, speaker identification) can be achieved.

ACKNOWLEDGEMENT

This book is developed from my six years study in the School of Foreign Languages of Shanxi University. This book cannot be completed without the assistance and help from many teachers and friends. A number of persons have helped me a lot in completing the study. I would like to express my gratitude to them, though it would be impossible to thank all of them respectively.

No acknowledgement can be sufficient for the debt I owed to my mentor, Professor Wu Yaxin, who has been guided me through not only the writing of this study, but also my academic pursuit and life ever since I fortunately enough was her student. I cannot help recalling the greatest experiences of my doctoral life under the guidance of Professor Wu. Whenever I have wracked my mind and heart for the study, she has been standing by me offering me elucidatory advice, informative suggestions and insightful comments. She has read every draft of the whole chapters of this study and given incisive comments, which allowed me to sharpen my analytical focus and improve the arguments made. The dense comments, suggestions and revisions are results of sacrifice of her leisure time too. I am grateful to her for her hard work, unending patience and confidence in me. It has been a great privilege and joy to study under her guidance and with her encouragement.

Moreover, she has shared with me her insight into the mission of a

ACKNOWLEDGEMENT

teacher. As she said, "For a scholar, the way to do research is the same way as to learn to be a man, a real man. We should not only be down-to-earth and positive, but also not be afraid of difficulties and setbacks.", "As a teacher, you should let students know the areas where they can improve in." and "As a teacher, it is important to make you (students) who you are today." She exerted herself tirelessly to encourage creative thinking throughout her lectures. It is her broad-mindedness and profound modesty that have made me understand the philosophy of life – to be too large for worry, too noble for anger, too strong for fear and too happy to permit the presence of trouble. It is her optimistic attitude towards life that has made me know how to appreciate happiness and beauty in ordinary life. It is her life philosophy of taking pleasure in helping others that has made me understand the joy of "giving a rose and retaining its fragrance". As she said, "We should cultivate good character, be generous and strive to benefit others and society." What I have learnt from Professor Wu is that I could never have learnt from anybody else. Her cautious attitude to research, immense erudition and personality will affect me for a whole life.

I am also deeply indebted to Professor Yu Guodong. His profound lectures have helped me improve myself and broaden my horizon. His enlightening instructions and experience in academic aspects bestowed upon me manifold insights and constructive advice. Needless to say, neither of these people is responsible for any errors. Those that remain are my own.

On 7th January 2015, these two professors established the Discourse and Interaction Group (DIG) by which they have been making great contributions to promoting Conversation Analysis in China and providing guidance to the young generation who find academic interests in Conversation Analysis. They have generously devoted their time and sapience, offering invaluable assistance to all the participants in the DIG. I would like to extend my gratitude to Professor Wu and Professor Yu for their selfless dedication.

I am also grateful to the members of DIG for their advice and encouragement along the way. My thanks also go to friends who helped me collect data and granted permission to use their data for analysis. Without their support, this book would not have been possible.

Finally, sincere and heartfelt gratitude goes to my family, including my beloved parents, my lovely sister, my aunt and uncle for their endless love, support and unwavering confidence in me. Their care and constant encouragement are the source of my strength.